→INTRODUCING

SLAVOJ ŽIŽEK

CHRISTOPHER KUL-WANT & PIERO

This edition published in
the UK and the USA
in 2011 by Icon Books Ltd,
Omnibus Business Centre,
39–41 North Road, London N7 9DP
email: info@iconbooks.com
www.introducingbooks.com

Sold in the UK, Europe and Asia
by Faber & Faber Ltd,
Bloomsbury House,
74–77 Great Russell Street,
London WC1B 3DA or their agents

Distributed in South Africa
by Jonathan Ball,
Office B4, The District,
41 Sir Lowry Road,
Woodstock 7925

Distributed in Australia
and New Zealand
by Allen & Unwin Pty Ltd,
PO Box 8500,
83 Alexander Street,
Crows Nest, NSW 2065

Distributed in the USA
by Publishers Group West,
1700 Fourth Street,
Berkeley, CA 94710

Distributed in Canada
by Publishers Group Canada,
76 Stafford Street, Unit 300
Toronto, Ontario M6J 2S1

ISBN: 978-184831-293-7

Edited by Duncan Heath

Printed by GGP Media GmbH, Poessneck

The most dangerous philosopher …

Dubbed by the American neo-conservative magazine *New Republic* as "the most dangerous philosopher in the west" and by the British *Observer* newspaper as "the superstar messiah of the new left", Slavoj Žižek is a radical intellectual and an outspoken public figure.

Žižek has gained his reputation as a polemicist. As the title to one of his recent books – *Living in the End Times* (2010) – indicates, his philosophical concern is with the widespread sense of impending world catastrophe and its underlying ideological causes. His work addresses the present political, economic and environmental global crisis.

The subject of several television documentaries, Žižek maintains a demanding schedule of sell-out public appearances and lectures across both Europe and the US that receive hundreds of thousands of YouTube views. With his work now translated into over twenty languages, no other contemporary philosopher can touch him for sheer popularity – even though his ideas are often complex and demanding.

What are the reasons for this popularity? Many people are eager to listen to a philosopher, such as Žižek, who has thought deeply about global problems of poverty, ecology and political repression.

I AM PREPARED TO OFFER NEW APPROACHES AND, WHERE REQUIRED, CLEAR SOLUTIONS TO THESE PROBLEMS.

This is a further reason why his ideas are so compelling.

The oratorical approach

Žižek has published numerous articles in journals and on the web, and over 50 books – at a rate sometimes of one book a year. Unlike many philosophers, Žižek's writing springs essentially from an oratorical approach to thinking and discourse, and this is part of his appeal both in hearing him talk and in reading his writing.

Žižek's process of writing is highly indicative of his direct approach to communicating ideas.

This method of writing has the added advantage of preserving the spontaneity of his thoughts, and it reflects his enjoyment in expounding ideas.

A native and lifelong resident of Ljubljana, Slovenia, Slavoj Žižek was born in 1949, when the small Alpine capital was part of Communist Yugoslavia. An only child, he grew up in the household of professional parents.

Much of his knowledge of Hollywood cinema – a subject he has written about extensively – was acquired during his teenage years, when he spent a lot of time at an auditorium that specialized in showing foreign films.

Psychoanalysis, the suspect science

As an undergraduate at the University of Ljubljana, Žižek did not support Communist orthodoxy and came into conflict with the authorities. Not sticking to approved course lists, he immersed himself in the works of Jacques Lacan, Jacques Derrida and other philosophers, mostly French, whose writings had found little favour in socialist circles.

> FROM OUR SOCIALIST POINT OF VIEW, LACAN'S WORK IS PARTICULARLY SUSPECT, BECAUSE PSYCHOANALYSIS IS PREOCCUPIED WITH THE SELF AND THE INDIVIDUAL MIND.

Žižek's eventual philosophical project became about reconciling psychoanalysis with collectivist politics.

Žižek earned a bachelor's degree in philosophy and sociology in 1971, and then pursued a master's degree, also at the University of Ljubljana, writing his master's thesis on the French philosophers whose ideas he had been studying. His research stirred up interest among the university's philosophy faculty, but its ideologically suspect qualities were more troublesome.

Although Žižek had been promised a job at the university, it was given to another candidate whose ideas were closer to the party line.

This opened up government speech-writing jobs, as well as the chance to take a job as a researcher at the Institute of Sociology and Philosophy at the University of Ljubljana in 1979. Žižek retained that position for the next several decades, even after gaining international renown.

The Society for Theoretical Psychoanalysis

In the 1970s, Žižek became part of a significant group of Slovenian scholars working on the theories of the French psychoanalyst **Jacques Lacan** (1901–81), and together they founded the Society for Theoretical Psychoanalysis in Ljubljana. This society, among whose best-known members are **Mladen Dolar** (b. 1951) and Žižek's second wife **Renata Salecl** (b. 1962), established editorial control over a journal called *Problem!*.

> I WAS NOT AFRAID TO WRITE BAD REVIEWS OF MY OWN BOOKS, OR EVEN TO WRITE REVIEWS OF BOOKS THAT DID NOT EXIST!

> WE ALSO BEGAN TO PUBLISH A BOOK SERIES CALLED "ANALECTA".

Žižek himself points out that the popularity of psychoanalysis in Slovenia owed to the fact that, in contrast to the other countries in the former Yugoslavia, there was no established psychoanalytic community to hamper or mitigate their interest in the usually controversial subject.

In 1981 Žižek left for Paris, where he studied with Lacan's son-in-law, **Jacques-Alain Miller** (b. 1944). Miller conducted open discussions about Lacan in Paris but he also ran a more exclusive 30-student seminar at the École de la Cause Freudienne in which he studied in depth the works of Lacan. Both Žižek and Dolar were invited to join this seminar, and it is there that Žižek developed his understanding of the later works of Lacan that still informs his thinking today. Miller also procured a teaching fellowship for Žižek and became his psychoanalyst.

11

Political engagement

Žižek took an active part in politics during the 1980s, a period during which Yugoslavia's Communist central government gradually began to lose control over the country's cultural life. He penned a popular newspaper column, and in 1990, when Slovenia was on the brink of independence from Yugoslavia (achieving it after a ten-day war in 1991), he ran for president of the Republic of Slovenia (a seat on the four-member collective Slovenian presidency).

It was at this time that Žižek's productivity blossomed, beginning with his first book published in English, *The Sublime Object of Ideology* (1989).

Presently Žižek holds a number of academic posts: at Ljubljana University, at Birkbeck College, University of London, and at the European Graduate Centre in Switzerland. Žižek maintains his right as an academic to pursue his research and his writing. This need to hold on to his intellectual freedom is a hangover from the Communist system, in which intellectuals were considered an important part of the theoretical underpinning of the state, and were thus financially supported if they were seen to be making useful contributions. Žižek cherished this freedom.

As Žižek's fame grew, he was frequently offered teaching positions in the United States, where he garnered a strong following in university cultural studies departments. He turned them all down, although he accepted visiting scholar appointments and often spent much of the year travelling from one academic centre to another.

The larger-than-life super brain

As a public persona, Žižek embraces provocation that is offset by a highly engaging and affable personality. He believes that the West has too readily dismissed the Communist era and speaks to Western audiences from an assumed position of inside knowledge on this subject.

Žižek's provocative side is counter-balanced by an astonishing knowledge of philosophy and politics and by an effective presentation of himself as a larger-than-life super-brainy intellectual exploding with ideas. While Žižek engages in polemics he sometimes intentionally evades open argument or dispute, a tactic designed to create a space in which the audience or interlocutor has to make up their own minds about their political and personal responsibilities.

Žižek's writings are primarily concerned with politics, but he often explores this issue through a wide range of topical subjects and interests. Just a few of Žižek's many interests about which he has written are:

Hollywood films (from silent comedies, especially those of Charlie Chaplin, through to some of today's popular box-office movies: Žižek is especially interested in the *Terminator*, *Matrix* and *Alien* series of films; Alfred Hitchcock's and David Lynch's films are also particular favourites).

Popular fiction (including Stephen King, Patricia Highsmith, Arthur Conan Doyle, Agatha Christie and Ruth Rendell).

"High" literature (Sophocles, Shakespeare, Kafka, Henry James, among others).

18th- and 19th-century opera (especially Mozart, Bizet and Wagner).

Biogenetics, neuroscience, and quantum physics.

I EXPLORE THESE SUBJECTS BECAUSE I BELIEVE THEY RAISE SERIOUS IDEOLOGICAL AND POLITICAL ISSUES. BUT IT IS ALSO BECAUSE I FEEL I CAN BETTER ENGAGE WITH PHILOSOPHICAL ISSUES **THROUGH** THESE SUBJECTS.

The idea of truth

Unlike many philosophers and intellectuals today, Žižek is not afraid of the idea of **truth**. Žižek's desire to speak of the truth is highly appealing and goes against the grain of recent intellectual and philosophical trends. When the German philosopher **Friedrich Nietzsche** (1844–1900) famously declared at the end of the 19th century that "God is dead", the idea of the truth – of some indisputable fact or reality – also fell into disrepute and became just as suspect as the belief in a set of God-given values.

After Nietzsche, what remained was the liberal notion that all values and beliefs, and their associated truths, are relative and partial: while belief systems may continue to exist, they are no more truthful than any other. But Žižek hangs on firmly to the idea of truth, despite the fact that it has become suspect and outmoded.

IN A TIME OF EXTREME SCEPTICISM AND OF LIBERAL VALUES, I INSIST THAT PHILOSOPHY IS STILL CAPABLE OF GRASPING THE TRUTH.

Power relations

By truth Žižek does not mean a spiritual or metaphysical idea of the truth regarding the existence of God, or a set of universal principles or laws that govern meaning and thought, as is traditionally the case in philosophy.

WHAT I MEAN BY THE TRUTH IS AN UNDERSTANDING OF THE REAL **POWER RELATIONS** THAT CONTROL SOCIETY AND THE **IDEOLOGIES** THAT PREVENT SOCIETY FROM REALIZING SOCIAL AND POLITICAL FREEDOM.

Essentially Žižek is a political philosopher committed to political analysis. He is intent upon intervening in political discourse in the belief that in this way he can affect people's ideas and help to change society.

As a way of describing the obstacles that lie in the way of achieving political and social freedom, Žižek likes to recount an old joke.

AN EAST GERMAN WORKER GETS A JOB IN SIBERIA. AWARE OF HOW ALL MAIL WILL BE READ BY THE CENSORS, HE TELLS HIS FRIENDS: "LET'S ESTABLISH A CODE: IF A LETTER YOU GET FROM ME IS WRITTEN IN ORDINARY BLUE INK, IT'S TRUE. IF IT'S WRITTEN IN RED INK, IT'S FALSE."

After a month, his friends get the first letter, written in blue ink:

EVERYTHING IS WONDERFUL HERE: THE SHOPS ARE FULL, FOOD IS ABUNDANT, APARTMENTS ARE LARGE AND PROPERLY HEATED, CINEMAS SHOW FILMS FROM THE WEST, THERE ARE MANY BEAUTIFUL GIRLS READY FOR AN AFFAIR, THE ONLY THING YOU CAN'T GET IS RED INK.

For Žižek, the joke encapsulates the underlying difficulties of speaking about the ideologies that establish everyone as **subjects** within society. A "subject" is someone who adheres to the rules and ideals governing language, communication and exchange ("the symbolic order") without being fully conscious of them.

Understanding ideology

By ideology Žižek refers to the way in which the fiction of self-identity is constructed through the structure of language and, more widely, the symbolic order.

IN ORDER TO UNDERSTAND IDEOLOGY AND THE DIFFERENT WAYS IN WHICH IT IS MANIFESTED IN SOCIAL AND POLITICAL DISCOURSE, IT IS NECESSARY TO REFER TO TWO KEY PHILOSOPHIES.

MARXISM, INSPIRED BY **KARL MARX** (1818–83) AND HIS INTELLECTUAL MENTOR, **G.W.F. HEGEL** (1770–1831), AND PSYCHOANALYSIS, INSPIRED BY LACAN.

For Žižek, Marxism and psychoanalysis share a common idea that absolute consciousness of the self is impossible to attain. Marx applied this idea to capitalism; subsequently, Lacan did the same in relation to the structure of language. Marx proposed that the subject is formed in the act of economic exchange (buying or selling commodities), while Lacan suggested that language constructs the subject as it speaks.

Many liberal and conservative writers and critics claim that these two intellectual traditions of Marxism and psychoanalysis are outworn and are no longer relevant to today's postmodern society. There are several reasons for this. Firstly, because Marxism is associated with the decline of Communism in the People's Republic of China, and in the Soviet Union and the Eastern bloc after the fall of the iron curtain in 1989. Therefore, Marxism is seen as something that belongs in the past.

SECONDLY, MARXISM'S CENTRAL CLAIM THAT POWER RELATIONS ARE FUNDAMENTALLY A MATTER OF IDEOLOGY IS NO LONGER APPLICABLE, BECAUSE WE LIVE IN A POST-IDEOLOGICAL SOCIETY.

David Cameron

Defending psychoanalysis

Popular mythology tends to portray psychoanalysis as something of a cliché, an indulgent pastime reserved solely for the rich and the upper-middle classes. Woody Allen's witty portrayal in his movies of New York's self-obsessed liberals points up this cliché. Žižek outlines three frequently recurring typical criticisms of psychoanalysis.

FREUD WAS OBSESSED WITH SEX!

DO WE KNOW THAT PSYCHOANALYSIS EVEN WORKS?

PSYCHOANALYSIS IS NO MORE THAN AN INTERESTING FICTIONALIZATION OF THE WAY OUR MINDS WORK.

The accusation that Marxism is outworn and that psychoanalysis is irrelevant to current concerns and interests is fiercely opposed by Žižek, who claims that these disciplines are relevant for understanding political unfreedom today as this is transmitted through ideology.

Against deconstruction

Žižek deliberately differentiates himself from other philosophers who he believes are incapable of breaking out of the ivory tower of rarefied intellectual ideas. In this regard, Žižek reserves particular criticism for the philosophical movement known as deconstruction that has been highly influential since the 1960s upon philosophical, literary and cultural studies. Deconstruction is especially associated with the French thinker **Jacques Derrida** (1930–2004), whose principal contention was that meanings are never stable and fixed.

Derrida was influenced by the Swiss linguist **Ferdinand de Saussure** (1857–1913) who observed that words have no intrinsic meaning. Thus, there is no built-in reason why a cat is called a cat or, indeed, anything is called by a particular name or word. The consequence of this is that meaning is endlessly "deferred" and can never be obtained. Meaning continually travels along the signifying chain.

IT'S LIKE SOMEONE LOOKING UP A WORD IN A DICTIONARY AND FINDING THAT ITS DEFINITION CAN BE FOUND ONLY BY LOOKING UP THE MEANING OF THE DEFINITION, A PROCESS THAT POTENTIALLY CAN BE REPEATED ENDLESSLY!

Žižek does not necessarily disagree with this analysis of language, but he is highly sceptical of the way in which deconstruction engenders a bourgeois and academic activity of writing *about* writing that is far removed from the world of politics affecting peoples' lives.

Crude thinking

Rather than a philosopher like Derrida, Žižek is more closely aligned with a thinker such as **Bertolt Brecht** (1898–1956), the Marxist playwright of the inter-war years in Germany. Žižek is especially drawn to Brecht's statement:

NOTHING IS MORE IMPORTANT THAN LEARNING TO THINK CRUDELY. CRUDE THINKING IS THE THINKING OF GREAT MEN.

For Brecht, "crude thinking" meant a form of political thinking that is direct and to the point. Brecht believed that his own brand of theatre (which he called "epic theatre") could awaken audiences to the truth and uncover the ideological conditions of class division. To some – including the Marxist intellectual **Theodor Adorno** (1903–69) – Brecht's didactic approach to the theatre was authoritarian. For Žižek, however, this is preferable to a detached and catholic approach to writing and philosophical thought.

Žižek the communist

Žižek's philosophy and ideas are formed from a position on the radical left of politics. Žižek is a self-declared communist. However, he is at pains to distance his ideas from the Communist doctrine associated with the totalitarian regimes of **Joseph Stalin** (1879–1953) and **Mao Tse-Tung** (1893–1976) in the Soviet Union and the People's Republic of China respectively.

INDEED, THE COMMUNISM OF THE 20TH CENTURY WAS A TOTAL FAILURE, ESSENTIALLY A CATASTROPHE ---

NOT JUST ON ACCOUNT OF THE SUFFERING INFLICTED, BUT ALSO BECAUSE OF THE INABILITY OF STALIN AND MAO TSE-TUNG TO MAINTAIN THE CAUSE OF POLITICAL LIBERATION BEGUN BY THEIR OWN REVOLUTIONARY MOVEMENTS.

The historical struggle for the commons

Besides his ongoing interest in the writings of Karl Marx and in the history of Communist developments in Russia and China, Žižek also retains a bond with the original semantic meaning of the term "communism" as derived from the word "commons".

FROM THE MIDDLE AGES TO THE 19TH CENTURY IN EUROPE, THE WORD "COMMONS" REFERRED TO THE IDEA OF COMMON LAND IN RURAL AREAS AND ITS COMMUNAL USAGE BY THE LANDLESS.

BUT IT ALSO CAME TO DENOTE THE HISTORICAL STRUGGLE DURING THIS PERIOD FOR THE RIGHTS TO SUCH USAGE.

While this struggle ended in ultimate failure in the face of the assertion of private land ownership, Žižek believes that the term "communism", if understood in its original dimensions, still has a strong relevance for developing an "emancipatory politics" today.

As a way of clarifying what is at stake in the common cause of "our shared social being" as this shapes emancipatory politics today, Žižek outlines three fundamental areas of social and political struggle:

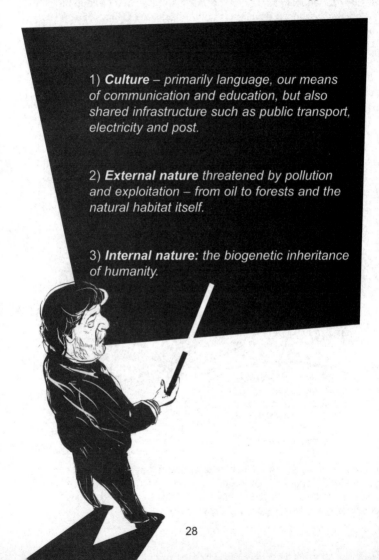

1) *Culture* – *primarily language, our means of communication and education, but also shared infrastructure such as public transport, electricity and post.*

2) *External nature* *threatened by pollution and exploitation – from oil to forests and the natural habitat itself.*

3) *Internal nature:* *the biogenetic inheritance of humanity.*

Collective change

Žižek's approach to these issues of social and political struggle draws upon his own political and philosophical background. Having been brought up in Communist Yugoslavia, Žižek retains a belief in social and collective programmes of political and economic change (albeit not necessarily of the type adopted in his own youth).

Because of his upbringing in Communism, Žižek has a special understanding of the Stalinist regime in Russia and Eastern Europe and, despite Western misgivings, he believes there is still much to be learnt about the nature of power and radicalism from this regime.

Repressive ideologies

As a philosopher, Žižek analyses present-day political conflicts and forms of ideological repression.

ONE OF MY PRINCIPAL TARGETS IN REGARD TO IDEOLOGICAL REPRESSION IS CAPITALIST IDEOLOGY AT THE LEVEL OF ECONOMIC EXCHANGE.

AND I AM PARTICULARLY CRITICAL OF THE IDEOLOGY OF LIBERALISM AND ITS PURPORTEDLY "ETHICAL" APPROACH TO POVERTY AND SOCIAL DESTITUTION.

Žižek's training in psychoanalysis also means that he is alert to psychological repression and the way in which the "super-ego" (otherwise known as the "big Other"; see p. 62) – the internalized authoritarian figure within the psyche – represses both the individual and society.

Ecology, the new opium of the people

Žižek identifies the issue of ecology as one of the most important areas of political struggle today. This is because of the growing global ecological crisis, and also because the major nation states seem so ineffective in stemming the crisis. In the face of this, Žižek outlines a radical approach as a means of remedy.

> TO BEGIN WITH, AN ENTIRELY DIFFERENT FORM OF THINKING IS NEEDED FROM OUR PREVAILING IDEAS ABOUT NATURE.

Concurring with the French philosopher **Alain Badiou** (b. 1937), Žižek believes that the dominant attitudes today towards ecology are deeply conservative, betraying an utterly naïve, almost spiritual idea of Nature. Adapting Marx's famous dictum, Žižek declares: "Ecology is the new opium of the masses, replacing religion."

Liberal ecology

Žižek argues that Christian and romantic ideologies still govern many of our ideas about Nature, especially those of the liberal class who take an interest in ecology. In these ideologies, Nature is seen as harmonious and beneficent; the earth is cast as "Mother Earth", a nurturing and benign figure. Today, however, it seems that the "natural balance" of the earth's biosphere has been profoundly disturbed by toxic waste and global warming.

THE TYPICALLY LIBERAL RESPONSE TO THIS DISTUR—BANCE SAYS ...

IN OUR EXPLOITATION OF NATURAL RESOURCES WE ARE BORROWING FROM THE FUTURE SO WE MUST TREAT OUR EARTH WITH RESPECT, AS SOMETHING ULTIMATELY SACRED THAT SHOULD NOT BE UNVEILED TOTALLY BUT SHOULD REMAIN FOREVER A MYSTERY.

For the liberal, it is as if global warming is a violation of the earth's sacredness. And, in being responsible for this, mankind is guilty. For the liberal, the lesson to be learned is that humanity must now tread very carefully in its treatment of the earth: "The lesson the liberal constantly hammers away at is our finitude: we are finite beings embedded in the biosphere which vastly transgresses our horizon. We must recognize that we cannot gain full power over our biosphere even though it is in our power to de-rail it and disturb its balance."

THIS CAUTIONARY APPROACH TO HUMANITY'S RELATIONSHIP WITH NATURE OPERATES IN THE SAME WAY AS RELIGION POSING AS AN UNQUESTIONABLE AUTHORITY BY IMPOSING LIMITS UPON HOW WE CAN CONCEIVE OF OURSELVES.

Nature the destroyer

Countering liberal ideas about ecology, Žižek points out that Nature is actually composed from vast amounts of destruction. On this subject Žižek believes that the theory of evolution proposed by **Charles Darwin** (1809–82) was wrong: "Darwin believed that the myriad designs of Nature are perfectly honed to do whatever they are meant to do: enabling animals to see, to feed and to take nourishment from the sun."

NO! NATURE TINKERS AND IMPROVISES, WITH GREAT CATASTROPHES ACCOMPANYING EVERY LIMITED SUCCESS.

INDEED, EVOLUTION IS COMPOSED FROM A SERIES OF CATASTROPHES AND DISASTERS, AND BROKEN EVOLUTIONS ARE PART OF OUR HISTORY.

AT EVERY POINT IN THE HISTORY OF NATURE THINGS COULD HAVE TAKEN A DIFFERENT PATH AND TURNED OUT DIFFERENTLY.

As a way of undermining these ideas, Žižek points out that the oil and the energy we rely upon is composed from a previous natural disaster of unimaginable dimensions. And he asks: If evolution is so perfectly designed, how is it that 90 per cent of the human genome is junk DNA? Adapting Lacan's audacious declaration, "La femme n'existe pas!" ("Woman does not exist!"), Žižek asserts:

NATURE DOES NOT EXIST!

Lacan's declaration was intended as a counter to patriarchal and idealized views of women; similarly, Žižek's intention is to offset sentimental ideas of a balanced world that humanity has disturbed but to which it might somehow return.

Facing up to radical contingency

Žižek understands very clearly the effect of the ecological crisis upon our sense of being in the world, and is very alert to the terrible impact of climate warming: "In it the very ground of our daily life is threatened, the most basic pattern and support of our being – water and air, the rhythm of the seasons of the year, and so on – this natural ground of our social activity appears as something contingent and unreliable."

The usual – liberal – reaction to the ecological crisis is to try to find a way back to "the earth's natural balance". But Žižek believes that this is a way of eluding the true dimension of the crisis.

THE ONLY WAY TO CONFRONT ITS FULL EXTENT IS TO ASSUME FULLY THE EXPERIENCE OF RADICAL CONTINGENCY THAT IT INVOLVES.

In Žižek's opinion, the lesson to be learned from the ecological crisis is that we must renounce all sentimental ideas about the universe: humanity does not – and never did have – a ground or a natural balance to return to. For Žižek, our existence is utterly contingent and beyond our control.

THE ECOLOGICAL CRISIS OFFERS THE MOST STRINGENT EXPERIENCE OF HUMANITY'S EMPTY AND MEANINGLESS EXISTENCE.

THIS IS IMPORTANT, SINCE IT STRIPS AWAY ANY RESIDUAL ROMANTIC OR RELIGIOUS IDEAS ABOUT OURSELVES AND THE ENVIRONMENT WE EXIST IN.

Furthermore, it enables us to confront global change and our own relationship to this – however drastic it might be – in a more open, flexible way.

IF YOU LOOK AT THE UNIVERSE IT'S A BIG VOID. THERE IS NOTHING. I MEAN IT QUITE LITERALLY. ULTIMATELY, THERE ARE JUST SOME FRAGMENTS, SOME VANISHING THINGS.

Concerning the question of how things originally emerged in the universe, Žižek agrees with quantum physics, "where the idea is that the universe is a void but a positively charged one. Particular things appear when the balance of the void is disturbed."

Žižek interprets quantum physics' "big bang" thesis as meaning: something went terribly wrong: what we call creation is a cosmic catastrophe, a cosmic mistake." This interpretation of the big bang fits very well with Žižek's own atheistic philosophy that is fully prepared to embrace a sense of the radical contingency of things.

Despite these dark views, Žižek is not a melancholic or an existentialist who dwells upon the meaninglessness of existence. He is an activist who believes that something urgently needs to be done about the ecological crisis. In Žižek's opinion, politicians are not able to accomplish this task effectively.

OUR PRESENT POLITICAL MASTERS CANNOT BE TRUSTED.

INDEED THEY USHER IN FURTHER CATASTROPHIC CHANGES BECAUSE THEIR MINDSET IS SO LIMITED, SIMPLY ADMINISTRATING THE SITUATION IN LINE WITH CAPITALIST INTERESTS.

Thus, Žižek believes our present difficulties call for extreme measures in the name of the common good and as a way of combating ruthless market forces that are deepening the ecological crisis.

Žižek's manifesto for the earth

To this end Žižek has drawn up an ecological manifesto boldly synthesizing into four points a robust programme of political change and collective action. Thus, he calls for:

"1) An imposition of world-wide norms of per capita energy consumption and carbon dioxide emissions; the developed nations should not be allowed to poison the environment at the present rate, blaming the developing Third World countries, from Brazil to China, for ruining our shared environment with their rapid development.

"2) Ruthless punishment of all those who violate the imposed protective measures, inclusive of severe limitations of liberal 'freedoms', and technological control of the prospective law-breakers.

"3) The deployment of large-scale collective decisions intended to run counter to the 'spontaneous' logic of capitalist development … to 'stop the train' of history which runs towards the precipice of global catastrophe.

4) AND, LAST BUT NOT LEAST, ALL THIS COMBINED WITH THE **TRUST IN THE PEOPLE** – THE WAGER THAT THE LARGE MAJORITY OF THE PEOPLE SUPPORT THESE SEVERE MEASURES, SEE THEM AS THEIR OWN, AND ARE READY TO PARTICIPATE IN THEIR ENFORCEMENT.

Poverty, the media, and "fair trade"

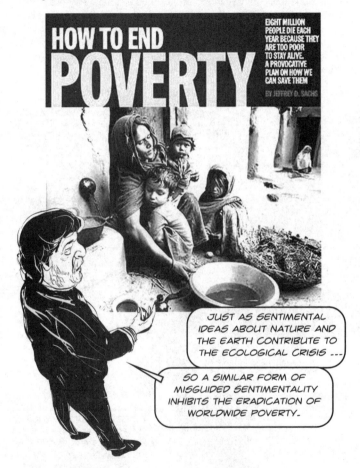

This issue is highlighted by recent shifts in modes of marketing by multinational corporations and businesses intending to develop, but also exploit, the increased desire among the liberal classes in the West to "do something" about saving the endangered planet and helping the world's poor.

Žižek recognizes that the principal way by which political opposition is mounted is through reacting to social inequalities as they are experienced, either directly or as reported through the media. It is especially owing to the media today in its role as a social conscience of global affairs that the liberal class has developed a keen awareness about poverty, both as this exists globally and also as an ever-deepening affliction in the West.

THE HUGE DISPLAY OF PUBLIC SUPPORT FOR THE LIVE AID CHARITY APPEAL IN 1985 WAS A DEFINING MOMENT IN THE GROWTH OF THIS AWARENESS.

Buying into anti-capitalism

It is exactly at this point of an increased awareness in the West of social inequality and poverty that Žižek identifies what he feels is a new, and from his point of view, worrying trend in corporate marketing strategies.

Many companies, of whom Starbucks are a prime example, now give a percentage of their product's cost to a recognized world charity or an organization working in the developing world.

ACCORDING TO THE COMPANY'S MARKETING, WHEN YOU BUY A STARBUCKS CUP OF COFFEE YOU ARE BUYING INTO SOMETHING MORE THAN A CUP OF COFFEE: YOU ARE BUYING INTO AN ETHICAL EXPERIENCE!

We are committed to helping the planet and to investment in the farmers who supply us with our coffee. Our aim is to encourage ethical trading and sustainable farming practices, building communities around the world.

A similar consumer pitch cited by Žižek is that of the American company TOMS shoes, whose slogan is: "One for one: With every pair you purchase, TOMS will give a pair of shoes to a child in need."

Redemption for the consumer

This combination of consumerism with an ethical dimension is, Žižek believes, "cultural capitalism at its purest – in the very consumerist act you buy redemption from being a consumerist". Žižek argues that this feeling of redemption from Western consumerist guilt is closely allied to the vogue for organic goods and other environmentally friendly products that also act as a salve to the consumer's conscience. Žižek caustically observes that when we purchase, say, a bag of organic apples, it is not because they necessarily taste any better than other apples.

IT IS BECAUSE IT MAKES US FEEL WARM INSIDE BY DOING SOMETHING FOR THE ENVIRONMENT, FOR MOTHER EARTH, FOR THE PLANET.

With the problems of poverty and ecology already included in the price of what we buy, our conscience is absolved. Thus, making it all too easy to think that capitalism takes care of the predicaments facing the world.

The disease of charity

For Žižek, this recently-formed bond between consumerism and ethical responsibility effectively nips in the bud a potential alliance between those liberals with a social conscience who wish to assuage poverty and the radical left opposed to capitalism. Furthermore, in Žižek's opinion, donating money to charities and other world organizations is not the long-term answer. Žižek concurs with **Oscar Wilde** (1854–1900) who argued in his essay "The Soul of Man Under Socialism" (1891):

Wilde suggested that charity is actually part of the disease it is trying to cure, since altruistic gestures simply preserve the status quo and prevent the radical reconstruction of society by which poverty may be alleviated altogether. Žižek's philosophy is that capitalism cannot be made to work for the good, however much it tries to put on a human face.

McWorld versus Jihad

Where he feels it is appropriate, Žižek analyses politics – especially
global power politics – not only as a matter of ideology but also in terms
of economic and market forces:

> SOMETIMES A DOSE OF ECONOMIC REDUCTIONISM IS VERY APPROPRIATE TO POLITICAL ANALYSIS.

In Žižek's view, the primary motivation behind the geo-political
manoeuvres of the US is to ensure the continuing domination of its
own capitalist interests. With this in mind, Žižek dismisses the supposed
opposition between Western "liberal" and Islamic "fundamentalist" values
as an ideological ploy fostered by the US.

What Žižek calls the "McWorld versus Jihad" conflict expounded by the media overlooks the geo-political adventuring of American-backed corporate interests intent upon gaining access to the Middle East's oil reserves.

For Žižek, the idea of a "clash of world civilizations", whether this applies to relations between the West and the Middle East or to other global conflicts involving the West, is not a matter of "us and them" but of Western interests in world affairs.

THE MOST HORRIFYING SLAUGHTERS – THOSE IN RWANDA, CONGO AND SIERRA LEONE – NOT ONLY TOOK PLACE, AND ARE STILL TAKING PLACE, WITHIN THE SAME "CIVILIZATION", BUT ARE ALSO CLEARLY RELATED TO THE INTERPLAY OF GLOBAL ECONOMIC INTERESTS.

According to Žižek: "Even in the few cases that would vaguely fit the definition of the 'clash of civilizations' (Bosnia and Kosovo, southern Sudan), the shadow of other interests is easily discernible."

The truth about the Taliban

In Žižek's opinion, the US military occupation in Afghanistan is not simply a "war on terror", since the war's causes go far deeper than this. Afghanistan was, until it became involved with the struggle of the superpowers in the 1970s, among the most tolerant and secular of Muslim societies.

KABUL WAS KNOWN AS A CITY WITH A VIBRANT CULTURAL AND POLITICAL LIFE.

THE APPARENT "REGRESSION" INTO ULTRA-FUNDAMENTALISM UNDER THE TALIBAN WAS THE RESULT OF AFGHANISTAN GETTING CAUGHT UP IN INTERNATIONAL POLITICS, AND NOT BECAUSE OF A DEEP "TRADITIONALIST" TENDENCY.

AND NOT ONLY WAS THE RISE OF THE TALIBAN A DEFENSIVE REACTION TO INTERNATIONAL POLITICS — IT ACTUALLY EMERGED DIRECTLY AS A RESULT OF THE SUPPORT OF FOREIGN POWERS (PAKISTAN, SAUDI ARABIA, THE USA ITSELF).

Žižek's conclusion is that the phenomenon of the Taliban should not be seen simply as a reversion to traditional, feudal values but more as a way of countering Western ideology and American imperialism. In other words, it is an outcome of contemporary political forces and not simply an overhang from the past.

As for the "clash of civilizations", let us recall the letter from the seven-year-old American girl whose father was a pilot fighting in Afghanistan: she wrote that, although she loved her father very much, she was ready to let him die, to sacrifice him for her country. When President Bush quoted these lines, they were perceived as a "normal" outburst of American patriotism.

Let us conduct a simple mental experiment and imagine: an Arab Muslim girl pathetically reciting into the camera the same words about her father fighting for the Taliban – we do not have to think for long about what our reaction would have been: morbid Muslim fundamentalism which does not stop even at the cruel manipulation and exploitation of children …

Murderous fanaticism? There are in the USA today more than two million Rightist populist "fundamentalists" who also practise a terror of their own, legitimized by (their understanding of) Christianity. (Žižek)

The paranoia of 9/11

Žižek sees the attack on the Twin Towers of the World Trade Center in New York on September 11, 2001 by al-Qaeda as a historic moment when the US, instead of seeing itself as a victim, might have begun to reflect upon its own imperialist ambitions and its disastrous consequences, of which 9/11 is only one aspect.

WE DO NOT YET KNOW WHAT CONSEQUENCES THIS EVENT WILL HAVE FOR THE ECONOMY, IDEOLOGY, POLITICS AND WAR, BUT ONE THING IS CERTAIN ...

Žižek believes that America was faced with two alternatives post-9/11: "Either to risk stepping out of its own sphere, or to strengthen the deeply immoral attitude of 'Why should this happen to us? Things like this don't happen here!', leading to more aggressivity towards the threatening Outside – in short: to a paranoiac acting out."

When Žižek is in an optimistic mood he envisages "America post-9/11 finally accepting that the attack on the World Trade Center was an inverted form of *its own* global violence".

THE TRUE LESSON OF THE ATTACKS AND THE WAY TO ENSURE THAT IT WILL NOT HAPPEN HERE AGAIN IS TO PREVENT IT HAPPENING ANYWHERE ELSE.

IN SHORT, AMERICA SHOULD LEARN HUMBLY TO ACCEPT ITS OWN VULNERABILITY AS PART OF THIS WORLD, ENACTING THE PUNISHMENT OF THOSE RESPONSIBLE AS A SAD DUTY, NOT AS AN EXHILARATING RETALIATION.

However, what Žižek sees happening in reality post-9/11 is a reassertion of "America's traditional ideological commitments and rejection of feelings of responsibility and guilt towards the Third World". According to Žižek, this approach is defended by the ideology: "*We* are the victims now and so we have every right to retaliate!"

Ideology and repression

Like other radical thinkers, Žižek's opposition towards capitalism lies in its creation of social inequalities, particularly as this is manifested in terms of the distribution of wealth.

But he does not believe that political opposition to capitalism can arise solely through an understanding of economics. For him, political and social repression, however manifested, is ultimately caused by **ideology**.

THEREFORE, MY PRINCIPAL TASK AS A PHILOSOPHER IS TO ANALYSE IDEOLOGY ---

PARTICULARLY AS THIS IS BOUND UP WITH THE FORMATION OF INDIVIDUAL AND SOCIAL IDENTITY THROUGH LANGUAGE AND DISCOURSE — THAT IS, "THE SYMBOLIC ORDER".

The symbolic order

What is the symbolic order? The symbolic order is both any **system of communication** (such as language, discourse, a method of monetary exchange, a game, or any system of signs) and the **rules governing that system**. Žižek refers to the game of chess to illustrate how rules operate in symbolic systems.

The same idea applies to language: "These are the grammatical rules which I have to follow almost blindly and spontaneously, and of which I am hardly conscious. If I were to bear these rules in mind all the time, my speech would break down."

Similarly, there are rules governing social interaction affecting politeness, friendliness and social space that in our everyday lives are not normally consciously noticed or considered.

There is also a whole set of taboos and prohibitions about what and when not to say or do something. For Žižek, submitting to the rules that govern language and the forms of social interaction is not a natural process.

THE ENTRY INTO THE SYMBOLIC ORDER IS NOT NATURAL OR INHERENT WITHIN THE HUMAN GENE CODE. THERE IS NO INBORN "LANGUAGE INSTINCT" WITHIN MAN.

The Trojan horse

Žižek believes that the symbolic order is a gift of communication for humanity. But it is also as dangerous to humanity as the horse was to the Trojans. It offers itself to our use free of charge, but once we accept it, it colonizes us.

IN USING LANGUAGE – WHICH WE DO ALL OF THE TIME TO COMMUNICATE AND THINK – WE ARE ESSENTIALLY UNCONSCIOUS BEINGS.

While we may be familiar with the grammatical and social rules governing language and communication, we cannot be conscious of all of them in the act of participating in communication.

Meaning and the symbolic order

Underlying all of the rules that govern the usage of any symbolic system is one fundamental rule or law: *meaning is dependent upon the symbolic system, itself*. And the paradox is that even if this dependency is recognized, it can only be done within the terms of the symbolic order.

However much we may strive to be conscious of our dependency and however much we may desire to represent our submission to the symbolic order, we cannot step out of it.

THE SYMBOLIC ORDER GOVERNS NOT JUST WHAT WE SAY BUT WHAT WE THINK.

INDIVIDUAL SUBJECTS EXIST IN AND FOR LANGUAGE AND THE SYMBOLIC ORDER, BUT NOT OTHERWISE!

The big Other

For Žižek, this constraint whereby the symbolic order governs the formation of the subject's own self-identity depends upon the rule of an authoritarian "super-ego". Just as the rules and laws governing the symbolic order are always present, yet cannot be acknowledged, so, too, this applies to the super-ego as an embodiment of these rules and laws.

Therefore, the symbolic order is composed of two elements acting in tandem: on the one hand, a subject who is formed through participating in the symbolic order …

A measure of the difficulty – even impossibility – of breaking free from the illusion of achieving reciprocity through language is the case of James Joyce's modernist book *Finnegans Wake* (1939). Joyce's text engages in a plurality of meanings and a multitude of historical and fictional references that seem to defy any rule or law. Nevertheless, the book is treated as if it is coherent, if only in terms of being a reflexive book concerned with language and meaning.

The emperor's new clothes

Žižek emphasizes the fact that the big Other is just as much a fiction as the symbolic order. "We all know that the emperor is naked in reality but, nonetheless, we agree to the deception that he is wearing new clothes by submitting to the symbolic order."

> WHILE TALKING, I AM NEVER MERELY AN INDIVIDUAL INTERACTING WITH OTHER INDIVIDUALS: THE BIG OTHER IS ALWAYS PRESENT.

> BUT EFFECTIVELY THE BIG OTHER IS PROPERLY **VIRTUAL**. IT EXISTS ONLY IN SO FAR AS SUBJECTS ACT **AS IF IT EXISTS**.

"Its substance is actual only in so far as individuals believe in it and act accordingly. Therefore, the big Other is also based upon 'lack'. Like the subject, its existence is merely an affect of the symbolic system."

Lack

Subjectivity is founded upon what Lacan termed a "lack" – the lack that is our unconscious. The unconscious exists as a blind spot in subjectivity: our inability to articulate and be fully conscious of our dependency upon the symbolic order. Thus, there is a void or nothingness at the centre of our being that effectively means our subjectivity is a void, a fiction.

"The symbolic order, society's unwritten constitution, is the second nature of every speaking being: it is here, directing and controlling my acts; it is the sea I swim in, yet it remains ultimately impenetrable – I can never put it in front of me and grasp it."

A universal system of exchange

In Žižek's view, the political economist Karl Marx's analysis of the capitalist economic system in his book *Capital* (1867) anticipated his own ideas about the symbolic order.

Marx pointed out that all economic systems, including capitalism, rely upon a single universal medium – in capitalism's case this is money – by which to gauge and evaluate all that can be exchanged and sold.

THE VALUE OF A COMMODITY ASSUMES THE FORM OF ANOTHER THING, MONEY.

The use of a single medium of exchange – money – subordinates every product, commodity and thing into one universal trading system. While this enables calculative exchanges to occur, it also represses the possibility of categorical differences between products, commodities or things. Marx's point was to question the viability of being able to comparatively evaluate products, commodities – including the amount of labour and time spent on making something – and things.

Marx believed that both traders and consumers under capitalism often recognize the absurdity of tying every product, commodity and thing into one universal system of exchange governed by the index of money. This absurdity is highlighted by the difficulty of how to adequately determine wages to workers and producers where questions of amounts of time, care, intellect, and mental and physical power exercised in the activity of work have to be taken into account and given a comparative price.

They do not know it ...

Nevertheless, while individuals may recognize the limits within the capitalist system of exchange and the inherent difficulties of calculating exchanges between products, commodities and things, this recognition becomes futile in the act of monetary exchange to which every manufacturer and consumer has to submit.

> THE PROBLEM IS THAT IN THEIR SOCIAL ACTIVITY ITSELF, IN WHAT THEY ARE **DOING**, INDIVIDUALS ARE **ACTING** AS IF MONEY, IN ITS MATERIAL REALITY, IS THE EMBODIMENT OF WEALTH AS SUCH.

To engage in monetary exchange is to uphold the symbolic system and, along with it, the big Other. Thus Marx said, in his famous definition of ideology:

> THEY DO NOT KNOW IT, BUT THEY ARE DOING IT.

Freud and the super-ego

The big Other is the Law underlying the symbolic order.

FIRSTLY, THE BIG OTHER IS THE LAW THAT COMMUNICATION AND EXCHANGE HAS TO PROCEED THROUGH THE SYMBOLIC ORDER.

AND SECONDLY, THE BIG OTHER IS THE LAW THAT THIS ATTACHMENT CAN NEVER BE FULLY BROUGHT INTO THE CONSCIOUSNESS OF THE INDIVIDUAL SUBJECT.

Žižek derives these ideas about the formation of the subject's identity through the big Other's presence in the symbolic order from his reading of Lacan and Marx. Additionally, Žižek holds to the psychoanalytic ideas of **Sigmund Freud** (1856–1939) that the big Other is a repressive force of moral authority affecting the subject's psyche.

Freud calls the big Other the super-ego, an ever-present figure of internal authority residing within each individual. The super-ego functions not only as a custodian of the symbolic order regarding meaning at the level of what can and cannot be said, but also it acts as a guardian of society's laws, morals and codes of good behaviour and proper conduct.

AS AN INTERNALIZATION OF THE FATHER—FIGURE AND CULTURAL REGULATIONS, THE SUPER—EGO CONTROLS OUR SENSE OF RIGHT AND WRONG AND GUILT.

Doing the right thing …

Žižek's insight into Freud's theory of the super-ego is that in obeying or transgressing society's laws and moral rules the super-ego always remains extant. And, so long as the super-ego exists, so too does the subject. Žižek's polemical claim is that it is the Law, itself, that generates the desire for its own violation.

THE DEVIL .

OUR OBEDIENCE TO THE LAW ITSELF IS NOT "NATURAL", SPONTANEOUS, BUT MEDIATED BY THE (REPRESSION OF THE) DESIRE TO TRANSGRESS THE LAW.

"When we obey the Law, we do it as part of a desperate strategy to fight against our desire to transgress it, so the more rigorously we OBEY the Law, the more we bear witness to the fact that, deep in ourselves, we feel the pressure of the desire to indulge in sin."

… for the wrong reason

"This Christian super-ego attitude is perhaps best rendered by T.S. Eliot's line from his verse drama *Murder in the Cathedral* (1935): 'the highest form of treason: to do the right thing for the wrong reason' – even when you do the right thing, you do it in order to counteract, and thus conceal, the basic vileness of your true nature."

In-built transgression

For Žižek, transgression – imagined or real forms of enjoyment that seem to contradict the dominant ideas or laws controlling social, moral and ethical behaviour – is built into all societies. This is because for every law or ideal of behaviour and conduct that exists in society, there is its implied crime or transgression that is prohibited or frowned upon.

THEREFORE NO POLITICAL REGIME, WHETHER TOTALITARIAN OR LIBERAL, CAN EVER SUCCEED SOLELY BY BEING REPRESSIVE.

And, indeed, in all political regimes and societies there is the tacit understanding that subjects can "let off steam" and enjoy activities that are not acknowledged in public life, such as telling dirty jokes, indulging in alcohol or drugs, consuming pornography, watching violent sports, visiting prostitutes and going to war.

The night of the world

Žižek's thesis, therefore, is that the super-ego, itself, is an obscene agency active within every subject. Žižek believes that this idea was already recognized by Georg Hegel in his dark vision of humankind – known as "the night of the world" – outlined in the *Realphilosophie* manuscript of 1805–06.

"The human being is this night, this empty nothing, that contains everything – an unending wealth of many representations, images, of which none belongs to him – or which are not present." (Hegel)

ONE CATCHES SIGHT OF THIS NIGHT WHEN ONE LOOKS A HUMAN BEING IN THE EYE – INTO A NIGHT THAT BECOMES AWFUL.

Hitchcock and the obscene

Žižek feels that a number of Alfred Hitchcock's films – especially *Psycho* (1960) – encapsulate the idea that every imperative upheld by the super-ego has its obscene counterpart. For Žižek, the three floors of the house on the hill in *Psycho* correspond to the three principal levels in the psyche of the film's protagonist, Norman Bates. The top floor = Norman's super-ego, the ground floor = his ego, and the basement cellar = his unconscious id. The interconnection between the first and last of these elements is shown in the scene when Norman takes his mother from the bedroom on the top floor of the house to the cellar in order hide her: her response is to berate him but also she takes this opportunity to flirt with him:

I WILL NOT HIDE IN THE FRUIT CELLAR! YOU THINK ME FRUITY, HUH?!

By not drawing a line or division between the super-ego and the obscenity within the unconscious, Žižek is fully prepared to accept that we are all implicated in the darkest of desires. This idea is made evident in another Hitchcock film, *Rear Window* (1954). Coping with a recent injury, Jeff spends his time observing the lives of his various neighbours opposite. At the same time, he tries to elude becoming sexually involved with his girlfriend, Lisa (played by Grace Kelly), telling her that he has no desire for commitment and marriage.

"What Jeff sees through the window are fantasies of what could happen to him and Grace Kelly. They could become happy newlyweds; he could abandon Grace Kelly, they could spend their time together like the ordinary couple with a small dog, yielding to an everyday routine that barely conceals their despair; or, finally, he could *kill* her."

As the plot of *Rear Window* unfolds, Jeff discovers that one of his neighbours has murdered his wife. In one of the final scenes Jeff is confronted by the murderer, whom he desperately attempts to stop by the dazzle of flashbulbs. Žižek notes that this scene "is shot in a remarkable, totally 'unrealistic' way".

WHERE WE WOULD EXPECT RAPID MOVEMENT, AN INTENSE SWIFT CLASH, WE GET HINDERED, SLOWED-DOWN, PROTRACTED MOVEMENT.

THE SCENE RENDERS PERFECTLY THE IMMOBILIZING EFFECT OF JEFF'S OWN FANTASY.

The murderer reflects Jeff's desire to murder Lisa. Far from drawing a line between hero and murderer, *Rear Window* reveals how the "hero" is the criminal he observes.

Kafka and the obscenity of the law

For Žižek, it was the genius of **Franz Kafka** (1883–1924) that rendered in literature the integral connection between the super-ego and the unconscious.

Kafka's subject matter was "the blind machinery of the law to which nothing is wanting, nothing is lacking". And yet this law is shown by Kafka to be inconsistent, based upon an arbitrary logic of enjoyment. Whereas the unconscious is often cast as a reservoir of wild, illicit drives, Kafka reveals how it is also composed of "fragments of a traumatic, cruel, capricious, unintelligible and irrational law text, a set of prohibitions and injunctions".

IN THE GUISE OF A FIGURE OF AUTHORITY, THE LAW IS ACTUALLY AN OBSCENE MADMAN LAUGHING AT US.

The Trial

In Kafka's *The Trial* (1925), the court scene featuring the struggles of the protagonist Josef K. exemplifies the law's lawlessness.

EVERY ATTEMPT TO ESTABLISH THE COURT'S MODE OF FUNCTIONING BY LOGICAL REASONING IS DOOMED IN ADVANCE TO FAIL.

"All the oppositions noted by Josef K. (between the anger of the judges and the laughter of the public on the benches; between the merry right side and the severe left side of the public) prove false as soon as he tries to base his tactics on them; after an ordinary answer by K. the public bursts into laughter."

"WELL, THEN" SAID THE EXAMINING MAGISTRATE, TURNING OVER THE LEAVES AND ADDRESSING K. WITH AN AIR OF AUTHORITY, "YOU ARE A HOUSE-PAINTER?" "NO," SAID K., "I'M THE JUNIOR MANAGER OF A LARGE BANK."

THIS ANSWER EVOKED SUCH A HEARTY OUTBURST OF LAUGHTER FROM THE RIGHT PARTY THAT K. HAD TO LAUGH TOO. PEOPLE DOUBLED UP WITH THEIR HANDS ON THEIR KNEES AND SHOOK AS IF IN SPASMS OF COUGHING.

Žižek notes that: "Further chaos erupts openly when the argument of K. is disturbed by a public act of sexual intercourse."

This relation between public law and obscenity is explored further through two comparable scenes in *The Trial*. The first is described by a priest in a short parable concerning a man from the country who wishes to gain entry to the law through a doorway; while in the second scene Josef K. finds himself in front of another door of the law: the entrance to the interrogation chamber. As in the first scene, the doorkeeper lets the visitor know that this door is intended only for him.

IN 1) WE ARE IN FRONT OF THE ENTRANCE TO A MAGNIFICENT COURT OF JUSTICE, IN 2) WE ARE IN A BLOCK OF WORKERS' FLATS, FULL OF FILTH AND CRAWLING OBSCENITIES.

"In 1) the doorkeeper is an employee of the court, in 2) it is a sexually provocative woman washing children's clothes; in 1) the doorkeeper prevents the man from the country from passing through the door and entering the court, in 2) the washerwoman pushes him into the interrogation chamber half against his will."

The first scene seems to suggest that the frontier separating everyday life from the sacred place of the law cannot be transgressed. However, the second scene totally contradicts this assumption and shows that while this frontier exists, it can be easily transgressed.

Modern or postmodern?

Although Kafka was writing at the beginning of the 20th century (he died in 1924), Žižek believes that his work is postmodernist and not modernist. According to Žižek, modernist literature is modelled around a fundamental absence of meaning. The prototype of a modernist text for Žižek is Samuel Beckett's *Waiting for Godot* (1948–49).

THE WHOLE FUTILE AND SENSELESS ACTION OF THE PLAY TAKES PLACE WHILE WAITING FOR GODOT'S ARRIVAL WHEN, FINALLY, "SOMETHING MIGHT HAPPEN".

BUT WE KNOW VERY WELL THAT "GODOT" CAN NEVER ARRIVE BECAUSE HE IS JUST A NAME FOR NOTHINGNESS, FOR A CENTRAL ABSENCE.

Another example of a modernist writer is **James Joyce** (1882–1941), in whose work each stable moment reveals itself to be nothing but a "condensation" of a plural signifying process.

"*Finnegans Wake* is of course an 'unreadable' book; we cannot read it the way we read an ordinary 'realist' novel. To follow the thread of the text, we need a kind of a 'reader's guide', a commentary that enables us to see our way through the inexhaustible network of ciphered allusions. Yet this 'illegibility' functions precisely as an invitation to an unending process of reading, of interpretation."

WITH *FINNEGANS WAKE* I HOPE TO KEEP LITERARY SCIENTISTS OCCUPIED FOR AT LEAST THE NEXT FOUR HUNDRED YEARS!

Postmodernism and presence

In contrast to Beckett and Joyce, Kafka's work is about presence – the presence of the dark stain of the law. For Žižek, Kafka's work is relevant to today because he recognizes that behind every form of enjoyment in contemporary society, whether sanctioned or transgressive, legitimate or illegitimate, there exists a super-ego directing it.

NOWHERE IS KAFKA'S INSIGHT MORE RELEVANT THAN IN THE CASE OF THE CHURCH – NOT LEAST BECAUSE, AS THE SAYING GOES, "THE CHURCH NEEDS SINNERS".

"The Church poses as a moral guardian of the people and as its conscience. Ostensibly, its message is one of abstinence: live a life free of sin, and control your carnal desires."

BUT UNDERNEATH THIS MESSAGE OF SELF–DENIAL THERE IS THE OPPOSITE MESSAGE: **PRETEND** TO ABSTAIN – AND YOU CAN HAVE WHAT YOU WANT.

"Officially the Church preaches prohibition regarding the seven deadly sins, but actually it is wholly dependent on these prohibitions being disregarded. The Church needs sinners who repent their sins."

For Žižek, the recent revelations concerning Catholic priests' involvement in paedophilia, and its cover-up by Catholic bishops, reveals what is already hard-wired into the Church's ideology.

Perversity of the Church

On an amusing but nevertheless pertinent note, Žižek illustrates the Church's perversity and its desire for what it prohibits with a scene from the film musical *The Sound of Music* (1965). In this scene Maria, played by Julie Andrews, presses the Mother Abbess to let her take her monastic vows.

BUT I TELL MARIA THAT SHE MUST RETURN TO THE EMBRACES OF CAPTAIN VON TRAPP.

AT THIS POINT THE ABBESS BREAKS INTO THE SONG "CLIMB EV'RY MOUNTAIN".

In the context of the film's narrative the song is (hilariously) full of sexual innuendo. At the same time the song openly contradicts Maria's yearning for abstinence.

The Church never existed

Žižek concludes from his analysis of this perversity that *the Church never existed*. This is because it relies upon an ideology that is by definition hypocritical and utterly ironic.

One of the principal political objectives of the Emperor Napoleon I in the early 19th century was to destroy the power and influence of the Church. This was symbolized at Napoleon's consecration in 1804. Rather than allowing the Pope to crown the Empress Josephine and himself, as was customary, Napoleon seized the coronets from the Pope and performed the coronation himself. Žižek imagines the Pope's response to this.

YOU MAY THINK YOU CAN DESTROY THE CHURCH, BUT IN ACTUAL FACT IT HAS ALREADY BEEN DEAD FOR 2,000 YEARS!

The Nazis' dirty secret

Žižek observes that there is invariably a hypocritical and contradictory character to the exercise of political forms of moral authority. In the case of the Nazis, a certain hypocrisy was upheld about their own obscene acts of genocide. The Nazis liked to maintain a moral image and insisted that their programme of exterminating the Jews and other dissidents was one of "purification". This is why they maintained the death camps as a secret, one that could be revealed only on condition that it was never acknowledged.

IN HIS SPEECH TO THE SS LEADERS IN OCTOBER 1943, HIMMLER SPOKE QUITE OPENLY ABOUT THE MASS KILLING OF THE JEWS AND OF WOMEN AND CHILDREN.

IT IS A GLORIOUS PAGE IN OUR HISTORY, *AND ONE THAT HAS NEVER BEEN WRITTEN AND CAN NEVER BE WRITTEN.*

Žižek observes that when codes like these remain under cover of night, unacknowledged and unutterable, it is their very unacknowledged status that reaffirms the group's cohesion.

At certain times in their history the Nazis, posing as the party of law and order, actually *required* their subjects to commit crimes while keeping this requirement an unacknowledged secret.

WE OSTRACIZED THOSE WHO WERE NOT WILLING OR READY TO UNDERTAKE THESE CRIMES.

Such was the case with the night pogroms and the beatings of political opponents after the Nazis' rise to power in 1933 during the period of national solidarity known as the *Volksgemeinschaft* (people's community).

The contrast with Stalinism

For Žižek, the mass purges and executions and the show trials of Politburo members carried out in Soviet Russia under Stalin's regime in the 1930s are a vivid example of the interrelationship between politics and obscenity. But this is not because Stalin's regime was necessarily "evil" like that of the Nazis. Žižek subscribes to a radical difference between Stalinism and Nazism. Contrary to popular belief, in Žižek's view Stalin was not intent upon ruthlessly realizing a project of total domination.

STALINISM HAD ITS ROOTS IN A MOVEMENT OF LIBERATION BEGUN IN 1917 BY THE PROLETARIAN REVOLUTION.

WHEREAS THE NAZIS WERE SIMPLY BAD GUYS DOING EVIL THINGS.

The obscene purges of Stalinism in the 1930s have both a tragic dimension and also a strangely absurd element, seen in the continual rounds of accusations of guilt and the series of political alignments and re-alignments that shaped the events of those years.

"If they did not arrest enough traitors and discover enough conspiracies, [the executors] were considered lenient and supporting counter-revolution; so, under this pressure, in order to meet the quota, as it were, they had to fabricate evidence and invent plots."

THEREBY EXPOSING THEMSELVES TO THE CRITICISM THAT THEY WERE THEMSELVES SABOTEURS, DESTROYING THOUSANDS OF HONEST COMMUNISTS ON BEHALF OF THE FOREIGN POWERS.

Žižek has personal experience of the Communist Party's hypocrisy. As a dissident in Slovenia, Žižek was treated with some suspicion by the powerful Central Committee, but he remained within the regime's power structure. Yet one of Žižek's colleagues, who fervently espoused the Communist ideology, aroused bigger suspicion and was ostracized by the Committee!

An excess of irrationality

Žižek maintains that Stalinism was more "irrational" than the Fascist violence. "In Fascism, even in Nazi Germany, it was possible to survive, to maintain the appearance of a 'normal' everyday life, if one did not involve oneself in any oppositional political activity (and, of course, if one were not of Jewish origin)."

WHILE IN THE STALINISM OF THE LATE 1930S, NOBODY WAS SAFE, EVERYONE COULD BE UNEXPECTEDLY DENOUNCED, ARRESTED AND SHOT AS A TRAITOR.

THE "IRRATIONALITY" OF NAZISM WAS "CONDENSED" IN ANTI-SEMITISM, IN ITS BELIEF IN THE JEWISH PLOT, WHILE THE STALINIST "IRRATIONALITY" PERVADED THE ENTIRE SOCIAL BODY.

"For that reason, Nazi police investigators were still looking for proofs and traces of actual activity against the regime, while Stalinist investigators were engaged in clear and unambiguous fabrications (invented plots and sabotages)."

Paradoxically, Žižek believes that this very excess of irrationality within Stalinism indicates that it was still in search of, or at least troubled by, an authentic form of liberation. "In contrast to Fascism, Stalinism was the case of a perverted authentic revolution."

THE VERY VIOLENCE INFLICTED BY THE COMMUNIST POWER ON ITS OWN MEMBERS BEARS WITNESS TO THE RADICAL SELF-CONTRADICTION OF THE REGIME ---

--- TO THE FACT THAT, AT THE ORIGINS OF THE REGIME, THERE WAS AN "AUTHENTIC" REVOLUTIONARY PROJECT.

"Far more than the gratuitous sadistic display of power, the Stalinist terror was an implicit admission of the inability to run a country through the 'normal' chains of administrative command."

The death of God

In Western society today it may seem difficult to identify the presence of a dominating super-ego, especially since society has moved away from Christian forms of morality towards secularism.

Friedrich Nietzsche

This put paid to the idea of a higher superior power, symbolized by the figure of God, controlling mankind's individual and social behaviour through an entire set of moral prohibitions and taboos, the basis for which are the Ten Commandments.

Following the idea of the death of God and the apparent loosening of moral injunctions within Western society, the Russian author **Fyodor Dostoyevsky** (1821–81) is, according to the existentialist philosopher **Jean-Paul Sartre** (1905–80), supposed to have declared:

IF THERE IS NO GOD, THEN EVERYTHING IS PERMITTED!

Žižek believes that this "freedom" to do as we wish never in reality overthrows the omnipresent figure of the super-ego. Even in states of apparent lawlessness such as that during the Bosnian crisis of the 1990s, the super-ego exerted a paradoxical power. Rather than forbidding permissiveness, the super-ego retained its authority by granting it: "If you follow me, you may with impunity rape, sexually harass, kill."

The myth of the permissive society

In the West, the idea of the "permissive society" emerged after the radical events and riots in European capitals in 1968 led by a mix of anarchists, communists and proto-hippies.

WE AIMED TO QUESTION CAPITALISM ...

... ALONG WITH IDEAS OF MORALITY AS TRANSMITTED BY THE NOTION OF THE "NUCLEAR FAMILY" WITH ITS EMPHASIS UPON SOCIAL STABILITY AND SEXUAL RESTRICTION.

But what, in fact, happened after 1968 was that its revolutionary ideas of liberation were re-appropriated by postmodern capitalism and flawlessly incorporated into its own ideology of apparent liberalism that pretends to be no longer strict and authoritarian.

Žižek believes that the idea of a "permissive" society in the West is largely a myth. It may be true that ever-new forms of perversity are indulged in, but this does not mean that society is hedonistic and free of moral injunctions. Whereas Dostoyevsky declared, "If there is no God, everything is permitted", Žižek subscribes to Lacan's riposte to Dostoyevsky.

IF THERE IS NO GOD, **NOTHING** IS PERMITTED!

Žižek's central thesis is that in a situation where everything is permitted, what in fact happens is an *increase* rather than a *decrease* in self-regulation.

Žižek acknowledges that the super-ego dominating Western society today is not what it was during the era of modernity from the late 19th century until the period immediately following the Second World War. In modernity, the individual was governed by the injunction to be a good citizen and ultimately, if necessary, to sacrifice one's life to the cause of the nation.

IN THE WEST THE IMPERATIVE WAS: "BE A GOOD DEMOCRAT!"

WHILE ALTERNATIVELY IN THE EASTERN BLOC IT WAS: "BE A GOOD COMMUNIST!"

In other words, the super-ego during this time was that of a paternal authority.

Paternal authority figures

This figure of paternal authority dominating mankind in the era of modernity corresponds to Sigmund Freud's psychoanalytic idea of the **Oedipal Father** ensuring that the subject acts in socially acceptable and meaningful ways (see following pages).

> BUT UNDER LATE CAPITALISM, SOCIETY NO LONGER MODELS ITSELF UPON A TRADITIONAL PATERNAL AUTHORITY OR SUPER-EGO.

Instead, a new form of the super-ego has emerged. Referring to Freud's ideas, Žižek believes that this is reflected in a shift from the figure of an Oedipal Father representing authority to a **Primal Father** of obscene enjoyment who symbolizes "authority" in postmodernism.

In his book *Totem and Taboo: Resemblances Between the Mental Lives of Savages and Neurotics* (1913), Freud postulates that within the pre-historical stage of human development – and, therefore, extant within today's social and collective unconscious – there existed a fundamentally different type of paternal authority from that of the Oedipal Father.

At this time the family or tribe unit – which Freud refers to as the "primal horde" – was controlled by a father figure who retained exclusive rights over all the females and drove away or even killed his sons who challenged his authority.

IN THESE CIRCUMSTANCES NO SOCIETAL "LAW" OF PROHIBITION EXISTED- RATHER THE PRIMAL FATHER RULED BY PURE FORCE.

Killing the father

How did the Oedipal Father come to take the place of the Primal Father, in Freud's view?

> JEALOUS OF THE PRIMAL FATHER AND HIS EXCLUSIVE RIGHTS OF ENJOYMENT, THE SONS DECIDED TO KILL THEIR FATHER AND (BEING CANNIBALS) EAT HIM.

However, following this act of parricide, the sons were overwhelmed by their new-found liberty and decided to restore the figure of a paternal authority to the social order in the form of the Oedipal Father, who prohibits the primal crimes of incest and murder. (This figure is named after the mythical Oedipus, who killed his father and married his mother.)

Enjoy!

Žižek believes that today the figure of the Oedipal paternal authority is no longer operative within society, and that an "obscene" Primal Father rules in his place, exhorting everyone to emulate him and enjoy!

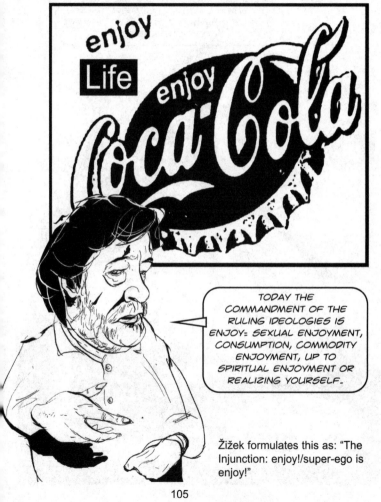

TODAY THE COMMANDMENT OF THE RULING IDEOLOGIES IS ENJOY: SEXUAL ENJOYMENT, CONSUMPTION, COMMODITY ENJOYMENT, UP TO SPIRITUAL ENJOYMENT OR REALIZING YOURSELF.

Žižek formulates this as: "The Injunction: enjoy!/super-ego is enjoy!"

Rather than forbidding the subject to indulge in immoral or excessive and perverse pleasures, which was previously the role performed by the Oedipal Father in the guise of the super-ego, Žižek observes that now there exists a pressure to fulfil such desires – as if this is the only way happiness can be found.

The ever-present object of desire

Today's commodity culture finds its perfect complement in a super-ego dedicated to enjoyment. Two principal ideologies are responsible for this.

THE 1960S COUNTER-CULTURE IN WHICH FREEDOM WAS EQUATED WITH PERSONAL, MORAL AND SEXUAL LIBERATION.

AND THE EMULATION IN SOCIETY TODAY OF YOUTH AND YOUTH CULTURE AROUND WHICH MUCH ADVERTISING AND MEDIA ATTENTION REVOLVES.

In the light of this, Žižek suggests that desire no longer revolves around an unobtainable, forbidden – and therefore, effectively *absent* – object of desire guarded by a prohibitive super-ego. Today's super-ego, with its demand upon us to enjoy, forces desire and its objects of gratification to short-circuit into an implosive spiral of addiction. Since subjectivity is equated with the fulfilment of desire, it is as if the absent object of desire has now become ever-*present*.

Simulated enjoyment

Inevitably, today's injunction to enjoy has its "fall-out", resulting in a pressure to look "good", to look healthy, to be young and, for women, to be slim and so on. The imperative is that you should be consuming, shopping, eating, having sex, etc. The logic of the injunction is that if you are not doing these things, then you are an unfortunate individual. The pressure to do more, see more, enjoy more actually makes people deeply unhappy.

As a way of contrasting how the Oedipal and Primal super-egos function within the psyche, Žižek is fond of telling a tale of two fathers asking their child to visit their grandmother on a Sunday afternoon.

IMAGINE A GOOD OLD-FASHIONED OEDIPAL FATHER. HE SAYS TO HIS CHILD ---

I DON'T CARE HOW YOU FEEL, BUT YOU MUST VISIT YOUR GRANDMOTHER: YOU HAVE TO GO, YOU ARE GOING. AND BEHAVE PROPERLY!

"But let's imagine a so-called tolerant postmodern father. He says to his child: 'You know how much your grandmother loves you, but nonetheless you should visit her only if you really want to.'"

109

In the first case the stakes of the imperative are very clear and explicit: the Oedipal law can either be obeyed or resisted. But in the second case this apparent free choice secretly contains an even stronger order.

This is an example of how apparent tolerant free choice conceals within it a stronger order.

Be true to yourself

In contemporary society under late capitalism one of the most familiar forms of the injunction to enjoy is a mildly hedonist injunction centred upon being true to yourself. This manifests itself in the desire to "make something" of one's life, to be "happy". Žižek sees this ideology of happiness as a Western version of Buddhism co-opted from the Buddhist pursuit of happiness. The West has adapted in its own image the Dalai Lama's philosophy.

THE PURPOSE OF LIFE IS TO BE HAPPY.

"Just how far this ideology has taken a grip in Western society is shown by the fact that in the US, courses in 'Happiness Studies' are now offered at some of its universities!"

The ideologies of advertising

According to today's ideology, the key to achieving happiness is through self-realization and by making one's life more "meaningful". This ideological tendency can be seen in recent changes within advertising. Traditionally, advertising had an **imaginary** and **symbolic** dimension. The imaginary dimension referred to the object's real qualities.

FOR EXAMPLE, IN ADVERTISING A LAND ROVER THE EMPHASIS WAS UPON ITS ENGINE POWER, THE ROBUSTNESS OF ITS DESIGN ENABLING IT TO GO UP STEEP MOUNTAINS AND NEGOTIATE ROUGH TERRAIN.

The symbolic dimension raised the issue of social status and "keeping up with the Joneses". In this instance, a Land Rover enabled the owner to appear macho.

However, a new dimension has appeared in advertising recently that centres upon the **experience** to be gained from owning the advertised product. This refers neither to the real qualities of the product (the imaginary dimension) nor to the social status to be acquired from owning the product (the symbolic dimension). This new dimension of advertising focuses upon how and in what ways the product renders one's life meaningful. The underlying message focuses upon this experience by asking implicitly …

DO YOU FEEL DEPRESSED IN YOUR LIFE?

THEN THIS PRODUCT OR LIFESTYLE WILL MAKE YOUR LIFE ENERGISED AND MEANINGFUL.

In other words, it is the experience that is emphasized.

Doing "good"

A similar tendency to seek a sense of meaningfulness underlies the widespread involvement, especially among the liberal classes, in so-called progressive causes today.

"Why do some of us like to buy organic food? It's not that it gives us a sense of social status. At stake, rather, is a pathetic and sentimental form of identification."

THERE ARE PROBLEMS IN THE WORLD: I PARTICIPATE IN DOING SOMETHING GOOD FOR THE WORLD, I DO SOMETHING TO CARE FOR NATURE — IT MAKES MY LIFE MORE MEANINGFUL.

Being involved in progressive causes offers the opportunity of an ethical experience: the belief that one is doing something "good" and caring for the world.

The removal of risk

A further reason why Žižek is suspicious of the equation that is made between happiness and self-realization in Western society today is how cautious and guarded people are about allowing any sense of intensity, risk or emotional excess into their lives.

These products are popular precisely because they are deprived of their malignant properties.

Taking these products as a prototype, Žižek envisages the future.

WE WILL SEE VIRTUAL SEX AS SEX WITHOUT SEX, OR WARFARE WITH NO CASUALTIES (ON OUR SIDE, OF COURSE) AS WARFARE WITHOUT WARFARE, AND THE CONTEMPORARY REDEFINITION OF POLITICS AS THE ART OF EXPERT ADMINISTRATION, THAT IS, POLITICS WITHOUT POLITICS.

In conclusion, Žižek states that: "Virtual Reality – computer simulated environments that compose new 'realities' – simply generalizes this procedure of offering a product deprived of its substance: it provides reality itself deprived of its substance; just as decaffeinated coffee smells and tastes like real coffee without being real coffee, Virtual Reality is experienced as reality without being so."

For Žižek, a supreme example of the way in which the potential excess existing within reality is transformed into a simulation of itself is the way in which the strike on the World Trade Center in New York on 9/11 was perceived.

"For the great majority of the public, the World Trade Center explosions were events on the TV screen, and when we watched the oft-repeated shots of frightened people running towards the camera ahead of the giant cloud of dust from the collapsing tower, was not the framing of the shot itself reminiscent of spectacular shots in catastrophe movies, a special effect which outdid all others?"

THIS IS THE ELEMENT OF TRUTH IN KARL-HEINZ STOCKHAUSEN'S PROVOCATIVE STATEMENT ...

THE PLANES HITTING THE WORLD TRADE CENTER TOWERS WAS THE ULTIMATE WORK OF ART.

Confronting the fictional subject

THE PROBLEM TODAY IS NOT HOW TO GET RID OF YOUR PROHIBITIONS TO HELP YOU ENJOY, BUT HOW TO GET RID OF THE SUPER-EGO'S INJUNCTION ITSELF.

So the question is: given the ubiquitous presence of the super-ego, or the big Other, can its repressive authority be overcome? Žižek's answer is yes. But he adds the proviso: only in so far as the subject is prepared to relinquish altogether their attachment to any kind of ideal and to confront the fact that the symbolic order through which identity is maintained is ultimately a fiction.

As an example in which this confrontation with the subject's own fictional status is taken very literally, thereby ending in tragic consequences, Žižek cites the late paintings of **Mark Rothko** (1903–70). These paintings are modelled upon Kasimir Malevich's "The Naked Unframed Icon of My Time" (1915), which consists of a simple black square on a white background.

THE BLACK SQUARE IS A SYMBOL OF THE VOID THAT IS THE UNCONSCIOUS, THE EXCESS THAT EXISTS WITHIN REPRESENTATION BUT WHICH CAN NEVER BE DIRECTLY KNOWN OR ACCESSED.

WHILE THE WHITE BACKGROUND IS AN OPEN SPACE IN WHICH "REALITY" IN THE FORM OF THE SYMBOLIC ORDER CAN APPEAR.

Mark Rothko

"All late Rothko paintings are manifestations of a struggle to save the central black square from overflowing the entire field. If the square occupies the whole field, if the difference between the figure and its background is lost, a psychic autism is produced. Rothko pictures this struggle as a tension between a grey background and the central black spot that spreads menacingly from one painting to another. In the canvases immediately preceding his death, the minimal tension between black and grey changes for the last time into the burning conflict between voracious red and yellow, witnessing the last desperate attempt at redemption and at the same time confirming unmistakably that the end is imminent."

Losing reality

It seems that to attempt to access the void that is the unconscious, as Rothko did, ultimately means to evacuate language and representation altogether. This results in psychic breakdown since language and representation bind together the subject. The conclusion would appear to be that without some artificial system of symbolic order by which to organize "reality", the individual ceases to exist.

FICTIONS STRUCTURE OUR REALITY. IF YOU TAKE AWAY FROM REALITY THE SYMBOLIC FICTIONS THAT REGULATE IT, YOU LOSE REALITY ITSELF.

Cogito ergo sum?

Nevertheless, Žižek holds open the possibility of the subject recognizing their own fictional status within reality. This is the ultimate purpose of treatment in psychoanalysis.

THE PSYCHOANALYTIC CURE IS EFFECTIVELY OVER WHEN THE SUBJECT FREELY ASSUMES HIS OWN NON-EXISTENCE.

Thus, psychoanalysis is the exact opposite of subjectivist solipsism (the sense that self-existence is the only verifiable part of reality) as proposed by the French 17th-century philosopher **René Descartes** (1596–1650) in his famous maxim: "Cogito ergo sum" ("I think therefore I am").

In the face of fundamental questions about reality and whether its existence can be proved, Descartes' maxim attempted to preserve the existence of the mind – that is, of a doubting, sceptical mind capable of thinking about the problem of existence and reality.

"In contrast to the notion that I can be absolutely certain only of the ideas in my own mind, whereas the existence of reality outside myself is already an inconclusive inference, psychoanalysis claims that reality outside myself definitely exists."

From S to $

By recognizing the fictional nature of unitary identity, the dominating presence of the super-ego is overthrown. In Lacanian discourse this is symbolized by the shift from the position **S** (representing the subject) to the position **$** (at the end of successful psychoanalytic treatment, the person analysed is "barred" from the fiction sustaining subjectivity).

BY SHIFTING THE "CENTRE OF GRAVITY" OF HIS BEING FROM S TO $, FROM THE SUBSTANCE OF DRIVES TO THE VOID OF NEGATIVITY, THE SUBJECT "RETURNS TO HIMSELF", THUS MAKING THE BIG OTHER SUPERFLUOUS.

The fiction of language

According to Žižek, the process by which the subject perceives their own fictional status, and therefore shifts from the position S to the position $, involves both a recognition that their own subjectivity is entirely fictional and void – based in nothing – and that this void is perpetually filled in by the fiction of language. And yet, while language conceals the void, it also *is* the void since it is an utter illusion – a symbolic system that generates the fiction of the subject. Following Lacan, Žižek terms this perception concerning the fictional status of language *'objet petit a'* (the small object 'a').

Like Lacan, Žižek posits the idea that it is possible to perceive or recognize the fictional status of language within which the subject is caught. However, this cannot be achieved through direct perception. In other words, direct access to the void that is both language and the void that lies "behind" language is impossible.

The perception that language is fictional can be achieved only through recognizing our perpetually misplaced belief in our own reality as this is structured through language and, more generally, the symbolic order and the big Other.

Optical illusions

In order to illustrate what such recognition involves, Žižek follows Lacan's ideas of the 1960s and 70s concerning the topology of "curved" space, exemplified by the Moebius strip. This is a strip of paper with only one surface so that its surface is effectively both one side and the other side at the same time! A model of the Moebius strip can be created by taking a piece of paper and giving it a half-twist, then joining together the ends of the strip to form a loop.

IF AN INSECT WERE TO CRAWL ALONG THE LENGTH OF THIS STRIP, IT WOULD RETURN TO THE SAME STARTING POINT HAVING TRAVERSED EVERY PART OF THE STRIP WITHOUT EVER CROSSING AN EDGE.

In other words, the recognition involved here is one of seeing that we were not where we thought we were, even though we remain in the same place.

Anamorphosis

Lacan's analysis of Holbein's painting "The Ambassadors" (1533) in *The Four Fundamental Concepts of Psychoanalysis* (1964) serves as a further example of what is involved in the recognition of our own fictional status. In the foreground of "The Ambassadors" there appears a strangely distorted object.

Seen from a high angle to the right of the painting, this object turns out to be a skull. This stretched illusionistic device is called *anamorphosis*.

When the illusion of the skull is perceived from the right of the painting, the image of the ambassadors becomes distorted and ungraspable. This contradiction reveals that the seamless field of the symbolic order in which the ambassadors are situated is a fiction and, ultimately, meaningless.

THROUGH THIS ANAMORPHOTIC DEVICE THE SUBJECT SEES NOT "THE VOID", BUT THEIR OWN BLINDNESS TO THE SYMBOLIC ORDER: THE FACT THAT THEY DO NOT SEE IT.

Buñuel and the desire for meaning

"Recognition" occurs at the point where the subject gives up the delusional idea that language and representation are the means by which to access meaning. The desire for meaning is simply a black hole, a condition organized by language itself. The film-maker **Luis Buñuel** (1900–83) plays on this idea through a series of never-ending postponements, as in *That Obscure Object of Desire* (1977).

A WOMAN, THROUGH A SERIES OF ABSURD TRICKS, POSTPONES AGAIN AND AGAIN THE FINAL MOMENT OF SEXUAL REUNION WITH HER AGED LOVER.

WHEN THE MAN FINALLY GETS HER INTO BED, HE DISCOVERS BENEATH HER NIGHTGOWN AN OLD—FASHIONED CORSET WITH NUMEROUS BUCKLES WHICH ARE IMPOSSIBLE TO UNDO.

"The charm of the film lies in this very nonsensical short-circuit between the fundamental impossibility of obtaining meaning and some trivial empirical impediment."

Buñuel's films hinge upon the fact that some everyday object or act becomes inaccessible or impossible to accomplish.

EL ANGEL EXTERMINADOR

ENSAYO DE UN CRIMEN

UN FILM DE **LUIS BUÑUEL**

THE NON—EXPLAINABLE IMPOSSIBILITY OF THE FULFILMENT OF A SIMPLE DESIRE REVEALS HOW THE UBIQUITOUS NATURE OF DESIRE IS WITHOUT MEANING OR PURPOSE.

"A whole series of films offers variations on this motif: in *The Criminal Life of Archibaldo de La Cruz* (1955) the hero wants to accomplish a simple murder, but all his attempts fail; in *The Exterminating Angel* (1962) after a party, a group of rich people cannot cross the threshold and leave the house; in *The Discreet Charm of the Bourgeoisie* (1972) two couples want to dine together, but unexpected complications always prevent the fulfilment of this simple wish."

132

Immoral ethics

For Žižek, there can be practical actions, deeds or decisions in life that implicitly recognize that the symbolic order is a fiction. Žižek says these acts fall into the category of "immoral ethics". By immoral ethics Žižek actually means, paradoxically, an **authentic** form of ethics.

IMMORAL ETHICS OVERTHROWS THE NORMAL COORDINATES OF THE SYMBOLIC ORDER AS THESE ARE GOVERNED BY THE BIG OTHER.

ETHICS IS ABOUT OUR RELATION TO OUR OWN DESIRE, AND OUR FIDELITY TO OUR OWN DESIRE.

Desire above the law

Much of Žižek's ideas on this subject of immoral ethics follow Lacan's discussion of Sophocles' play *Antigone* (c. 442 BC) in his 1959–60 seminar published in *The Ethics of Psychoanalysis*.

In the play, Antigone stubbornly defies the edict of Creon, King of Thebes, to leave the body of her brother, Polyneices, lying dishonoured on the battlefield. She buries her brother in the knowledge that she will be punished and buried alive.

ANTIGONE'S DESIRE TO HONOUR HER BROTHER IS ABOVE THE LAW.

IN DEFYING THE LAW, ANTIGONE SHOWS THAT THE ONLY THING OF WHICH ONE CAN BE GUILTY IS HAVING GIVEN GROUND RELATIVE TO ONE'S DESIRE.

Žižek agrees, stating that ethics is about our relation to our own desire.

Immoral ethical acts such as that of Antigone challenge not just the ideals of the big Other but also the subject's very identity and assumptions. To illustrate this, Žižek refers to a scene in David Fincher's film *Fight Club* (1999) in which the narrator hits and punches himself in front of his boss.

"Far from standing for some form of masochism or perverted form of violence, this scene is deeply liberating. I'm here, as it were, on the side of the fist. This is what liberation means: in order to attack the enemy, you first have to beat the shit out of yourself, to get rid of that which is in yourself that attaches you to the leader, to slavery and so on."

Refusal of dialogue

An "immoral ethical" act can take the form of a rebellious refusal. As economic recession hit the West from 2008 onwards, politicians began to increase taxation, cut benefits and dismantle the welfare state. In this situation, politicians are apt to endorse their actions with the appeal to society.

WE ARE ALL IN THIS TOGETHER!

PLEAS HELP ME I am POOR And SICK I WILL VOTE FOR YOU THANK YOU

David Cameron

*WE ARE **NOT** ALL IN THIS TOGETHER, FOR THE SIMPLE REASON THAT POLITICIANS TODAY CANNOT BE TRUSTED TO HANDLE THE CRISIS.*

Indeed, in Žižek's view, politicians deepen the crisis by attempting to administrate it in line with capitalist interests.

In such a political and economic crisis, Žižek conjectures that the appropriate action might be for the people to cease dialogue with politicians altogether – an idea prompted by a scene from Bertolucci's 1976 film *Novecento* (*1900*). In this scene a landowner speaks to a group of farm labourers, defending cutbacks by saying: "I'm making sacrifices, too!" At which point one of the labourers brutally cuts off his own ear in a violent declaration that he and his companions will listen no longer.

From this scene Žižek concludes two points: 1) Sometimes dialogue is not appropriate in situations of conflict, even though this is thought by capitalists to be essential to political progress. 2) The struggle for liberation from oppression is often of necessity a painful process (although Žižek is not necessarily advocating that we should all cut off our ears!).

Immoral ethics in *Don Giovanni* ...

Žižek stresses that his idea of immoral ethics is not a matter of fulfilling one's fantasies of desire, for instance of an unrestrained hedonism.

DESIRE DOES NOT MEAN FOLLOWING YOUR NATURAL, SPONTANEOUS INCLINATIONS. DESIRE MEANS YOU FOLLOW IT EVEN IF IT BRINGS PAIN.

To gauge this further, Žižek offers an unusual interpretation of the character of the eponymous "hero" in Mozart's opera *Don Giovanni* (1787).

Giovanni is a young, licentious nobleman who abuses women and ...ages society. At the end of the opera, when confronted by the ...mmendatore", a statue representing ...al conscience, and ordered to ...nt, Don Giovanni refuses ...n though he knows ...ill burn in hell. ...k asks why ...s Don ...vanni ...repent?

OBVIOUSLY NOT FOR LATER PROFIT. BUT OUT OF AN UTMOST FIDELITY TO THE LIFE HE FOLLOWED.

HOWEVER IMMORAL THE LIFE HE LED, IT WAS NOT FOR PLEASURE OR PROFIT BUT TO FOLLOW HIS OWN PRINCIPLES. OUT OF AN EXISTENTIAL CHOICE.

… and *Carmen*

A similar example is the character of the beautiful romany woman
Carmen from Bizet's opera of the same name (1875). Like Don Giovanni,
Carmen is "immoral", and in following her own desire she ends up
ruining her lover's life. After seducing Don José and getting him to desert
the army, she throws him over for a matador: as the libretto states: "free
she was born and free she will die". Out of jealousy, Don José murders
Carmen.

CARMEN'S BEHAVIOUR
IS TRULY ETHICAL: SHE
FOLLOWS HER PATH TO
THE END, EVEN THOUGH IT
MEANS HER OWN DEATH
AND IN THE PROCESS
DESTROYING ANOTHER
MAN'S LIFE.

Revolutionary ethics

Lacan's analysis of *Antigone* provides a model for Žižek's ideas about an immoral ethics as this applies to individual acts.

HOWEVER, THE ESSENCE OR SPIRIT OF AN IMMORAL ETHICS IS ALSO AT STAKE IN COLLECTIVE ACTIONS, ESPECIALLY REVOLUTIONARY EVENTS.

In this respect, Žižek is particularly interested in the events of the French revolution between 1789 and 1793, the Russian revolution from 1917 to the 1930s, and the Maoist revolution in China beginning in the 1920s and ending with Mao Tse-Tung's death in 1976.

Terror as virtue

With regard to the French revolution, Žižek extends the application of ethics as "fidelity to our own desire" not just to the initial founding moments of the revolution with the Declaration of the Rights of Man and the Citizen in 1789, but also to the so-called "Reign of Terror" launched by the Jacobin leader **Maximilien Robespierre** (1758–94) from 1793 to 1794. The Terror began with the execution of King Louis XVI and his wife Marie-Antoinette.

BUT IT EXTENDED TO A FURTHER 16,594 DEATHS OF COUNTER-REVOLUTIONARIES BY GUILLOTINE AND AN ESTIMATED 40,000 SUMMARY EXECUTIONS OF POLITICAL PRISONERS ...

INCLUDING FINALLY ROBESPIERRE HIMSELF.

Žižek opposes the typical liberal attitude towards the French revolution whose formula, as he sees it, is "1789 without 1793": "In short, what the sensitive liberals want is a decaffeinated revolution, a revolution which doesn't smell of revolution."

Robespierre's proclaimed goal was "to return the destiny of liberty into the hands of the truth". And to this end, nothing – not even the punishment and merciless death of counter-revolutionaries – was allowed to stand in the way.

Žižek takes up Robespierre's point: "Moderates want a revolution deprived of the excess in which terror and democracy coincide, a revolution respecting social rules, subordinated to pre-existing norms, a revolution in which violence is deprived of the 'divine' dimension and thus reduced to a strategic intervention serving precise and limited goals."

A decision made in solitude

The "divine dimension" in this context of revolutionary violence does not refer to a transcendental dimension, an intervention by a god or supernatural deity who wreaks vengeance upon the oppressors and the corrupt. Instead Žižek views it as "the heroic assumption of the solitude of a sovereign decision. It is a decision (to kill, to risk or lose one's life) made in absolute solitude, not covered by the big Other."

Quoting Robespierre, Žižek believes that there is a point in revolutionary events – including that of the Terror – where justice and vengeance can coincide.

TRUTH UNDOUBTEDLY HAS ITS POWER, IT HAS ITS ANGER, ITS OWN DESPOTISM. IT HAS TOUCHING ACCENTS AND TERRIBLE ONES, THAT RESOUND WITH FORCE IN PURE HEARTS AS IN GUILTY CONSCIENCES.

Beyond good and evil

For Žižek, an excess existing beyond any pre-established forms of morality or laws is a hallmark of true revolutionary politics. Therefore, in an authentic revolution there is no question of its participants being either innocent or guilty, since no state or law exists by which to measure such standards. In a revolution everything is overthrown, including the idea that there is an independent way of judging what is right and what is wrong.

THE DIFFERENCE BETWEEN LEGITIMATE AND ILLEGITIMATE STATE POWER IS SUSPENDED – THAT IS, THE POINT AT WHICH STATE POWER *AS SUCH* IS ILLEGITIMATE.

Žižek believes that these ideas accord with Friedrich Nietzsche's aptly titled book, *Beyond Good and Evil* (1886).

Žižek interprets Robespierre's declaration in 1792 that the trial of King Louis was not a trial at all as an assertion that the true revolutionary state exists beyond ideas of good and evil.

Robespierre went on to say that King Louis' execution was fitting because he opposed the revolution and not because he was guilty, as such: "Louis was king, and the Republic is founded: the famous question you are considering is settled by those words alone. Louis was dethroned by his crimes; Louis denounced the French people as rebellious; to chastise it, he called on the arms of his fellow tyrants; victory and the people decided that he was the rebellious one."

THEREFORE LOUIS CANNOT BE JUDGED: EITHER HE IS ALREADY CONDEMNED OR THE REPUBLIC IS NOT ACQUITTED.

Change at any cost

Žižek observes that "the true problem of revolution is not taking power; it's what you do the day after". In Žižek's view, the Reign of Terror was an attempt to maintain the revolutionary event of 1789, and not deny it, by fully embracing the need to change the existing social relations of power at any cost. Another example of such change in Žižek's view was Stalin's – ultimately failed – attempt in Russia during the late 1920s to collectivize the peasantry and destroy the existing feudal methods of organizing labour.

THE PEASANTS MADE UP 80 PER CENT OF THE RUSSIAN POPULATION AT THE TIME. STALIN TRULY WANTED TO BREAK THE PEASANTS.

THAT WAS TRUE VIOLENCE, IF BY VIOLENCE YOU MEAN CHANGING THE BASIC SOCIAL INFRASTRUCTURE, THE FUNDAMENTAL RELATIONS OF SOCIETY.

Re-evaluating Stalin

Žižek acknowledges that by the early 1930s Stalin's radical political project had more or less imploded (although certain traces of the original revolutionary spirit remained). Nevertheless, as with Robespierre, Žižek is concerned to re-evaluate aspects of Stalin's politics and not simply condemn it outright.

ONE EXAMPLE OF THIS IS THAT STALIN CLEARLY UNDERSTOOD THE IDEA OF REMAINING TRUE TO ONE'S OWN DESIRE.

Stalin owned Lenin's book *Materialism and Empirio-Criticism* (1908), a copy of which was found in Stalin's bedroom after his death. On the back cover Stalin wrote in red pencil:

First weakness, second idleness and third, stupidity. These are the only things that can be called vices. Everything else to the absence of the aforementioned is undoubtedly virtue. If a man is firstly strong spiritually, secondly active and thirdly clever or capable, then he is good regardless of any other vices.

In Žižek's view, this summarizes very well his own notion of "immoral ethics".

Violence and impotence

As an example of a recent political event enacting the violence of immoral ethics, Žižek refers to the food riots in Rio de Janeiro in the 1990s, when the people of the impoverished *favelas* descended into the city and began to loot and terrorize the middle classes.

However, Žižek is concerned not to advocate violence simply for its own sake.

THE QUESTION IS, AS ALWAYS, THAT OF TEMPORALITY, OF TIMING.

"The task of the revolutionary is indeed to be violent, but also to avoid the type of violence that is, in fact, merely an impotent *passage à l'acte* [an impulsive acting out]. Often the most brutal explosions of violence are admissions of impotence."

In the light of this recognition, Žižek believes that "there are moments when the radical gesture is to do nothing".

No compromise with the big Other

Whatever the form that radical gestures of political liberation may take – a riot, a lynching, an outright refusal to engage in political discourse, an imposition of collective or statist will – Žižek claims that such gestures render the big Other redundant.

I FIRMLY DISAGREE WITH THE ARGUMENT THAT TO FOLLOW ONE'S OWN DESIRE IS STILL TO ACCEDE TO THE LAW OF THE BIG OTHER IN THE FORM OF THE *RULE* OF ONE'S OWN DESIRE.

According to Žižek: "Lacan's maxim of the ethics of psychoanalysis – 'not to compromise one's desire' – is not to be confused with the pressure of the super-ego. Nor is renouncing enjoyment a compromise with the super-ego's command 'Enjoy'."

THE ONLY COMPROMISE IS TO BE GUILTY OF NOT FOLLOWING OUR DESIRE.

SUCH A COMPROMISE IS THE WAY THE SUPER-EGO GETS HOLD OF US AND LIKE AN EXTORTIONER SLOWLY BLEEDS US TO DEATH.

DESIRE

Duty and the categorical imperative

Like Lacan, Žižek refers to the Enlightenment philosopher **Immanuel Kant** (1724–1804) and his concept of the "categorical imperative" developed in the *Critique of Practical Reason* (1788) as a way of understanding the non-relation between following one's desire and the super-ego.

Kant's categorical imperative resides in the unconditional injunction to do our duty: "You can, because you must!" This leaves open the question: "What is my duty?"

WHATEVER I DECIDE TO BE MY DUTY *IS* MY DUTY.

THE SUBJECT HERSELF HAS TO ASSUME THE RESPONSIBILITY OF TRANSLATING THE ABSTRACT INJUNCTION "YOU CAN, BECAUSE YOU MUST!" INTO A SERIES OF CONCRETE OBLIGATIONS.

By refusing to identify *a priori* (in advance) what duty is, Kant ensured that it cannot be made into an excuse by which to avoid one's responsibility. On this point, Žižek takes issue with Adolf Eichmann's defence in 1961 of his Nazi past (as an SS officer, Eichmann was one of the principal organizers of the deportation of the Jews to the concentration camps).

Kant's answer to this kind of defence was that "There is no excuse for accomplishing one's duty". In other words, as Žižek states, "the reference to duty as the excuse to do one's duty is hypocritical".

Following this line of thinking, Žižek offers another comparable example: "Recall the proverbial example of a severe and sadistic teacher who subjects his pupils to merciless discipline and torture; his excuse to himself and to others is ..."

I MYSELF FIND IT HARD TO EXERT SUCH PRESSURE ON THE POOR KIDS, BUT WHAT CAN I DO — IT'S MY DUTY!

TO THIS, I REPLY: I AM FULLY RESPONSIBLE NOT ONLY FOR DOING MY DUTY, BUT NO LESS FOR DETERMINING **WHAT** MY DUTY IS.

In other words, the responsibility for any crime committed in the name of duty must remain fairly and squarely with the subject: it cannot be blamed on some figure of the big Other.

A further consequence of removing responsibility for one's actions from the fantasized support of the big Other is that the subject cannot excuse his or her actions by claiming they were powerless to defy the authorities. "Take the example of the concentration camp guards or of a torturer; such a person cannot remove themselves from their acts, justifying them by saying: 'I am only doing my duty'."

YOU MUST ASSUME NOT ONLY RESPONSIBILITY FOR YOUR DUTY BUT ALSO FULL RESPONSIBILITY FOR WHAT YOUR DUTY IS.

YOU CANNOT SAY, "I CANNOT HELP IT, I WAS SIMPLY DOING WHAT I WAS TOLD". OR, IT WAS MY UNCONSCIOUS THAT LED ME TO DO IT: *YOU CAN HELP IT!*

Following Lacan, Žižek claims that the subject is responsible even for their own unconscious, since that is where their desire is situated.

159

There is no big Other

The implication of Žižek's arguments about duty is that the subject has to assume entire responsibility for his or her actions. Žižek subscribes to Lacan's view that "there is no big Other": the big Other is a total fantasy. For this reason, Žižek disagrees with the ethics of "infinite judgement" as proposed by the philosopher Jacques Derrida.

WE MUST ACT IN THE PRESENT AS IF WE WILL BE JUDGED RETROACTIVELY IN THE FUTURE BY A COMMUNITY THAT IS LIBERATED AND FREE.

Žižek refutes this idea, since it maintains the idea of a big Other who, while not existing in the present, still exerts an influence upon the present from a – yet to be decided – future.

The big Other and the Bible

Žižek claims that the realisation that "there is no big Other, no Father up there to take care of things" is actually an idea that is explored in the Bible. In Žižek's opinion, the Book of Job is a riddle that strikes a dissonant chord in the Old Testament, and that therefore needs to be approached in the manner of a philosophical text rather than a religious one.

INSTEAD OF REJOICING IN THE OMNIPOTENCE OF GOD AND THE INSIGNIFICANT STATUS OF MANKIND LIKE THE OTHER TEXTS IN THE OLD TESTAMENT, THE BOOK OF JOB QUESTIONS THE VERY PURPOSE OF GOD.

Despite the fact that Job believed in God and was a very pious man, nevertheless, he experienced a series of personal disasters.

In the book, a visit by three friends – Eliphaz the Temanite, Bildad the Shuhite and Zophar the Naamathite – becomes the occasion for speculation about God's reasons for harming Job, and God himself eventually takes a part in this discussion.

For Žižek, "The true surprise is that the Book of Job does not provide a satisfying answer to the riddle of Job's plight".

JOB IS NOT TOLD THAT HIS MISFORTUNES WERE DUE TO HIS SINS OR A PART OF ANY PLAN FOR HIS IMPROVEMENT.

GOD COMES IN AT THE END NOT TO ANSWER RIDDLES BUT TO PROPOUND THEM.

God's refusal to explain His design would seem to support the orthodox biblical idea that his divine work is beyond mankind's comprehension. But Žižek believes that God's insistence upon the inexplicableness of everything in the Book of Job has more surprising consequences.

GOD WILL MAKE JOB SEE A STARTLING UNIVERSE IF HE CAN ONLY DO IT BY MAKING JOB SEE AN IDIOTIC UNIVERSE.

TO STARTLE MAN, GOD BECOMES FOR AN INSTANT A BLASPHEMER. ONE MIGHT ALMOST SAY THAT GOD BECOMES FOR AN INSTANT AN *ATHEIST*.

"[God] unrolls before Job a long panorama of created things: the horse, the eagle, the raven, the wild ass, the peacock, the ostrich, the crocodile. He so describes each of them that it sounds like a monster walking in the sun."

THE WHOLE IS A SORT OF PSALM OR RHAPSODY OF THE SENSE OF WONDER.

THE MAKER OF ALL THINGS IS ASTONISHED AT THE THINGS HE HAS HIMSELF MADE.

Žižek claims that in the Book of Job the figure of God goes against every assumption of logical or coherent argument, thereby plunging meaning into an abyss. "Job puts forward a note of interrogation; God answers with a note of exclamation."

INSTEAD OF PROVING TO JOB THAT IT IS AN EXPLICABLE WORLD, HE INSISTS THAT IT IS A MUCH STRANGER WORLD THAN JOB EVER THOUGHT IT WAS.

"God resolves the riddle, supplanting it with an even more radical riddle, and so by way of redoubling the riddle he, himself, comes to share Job's astonishment at the chaotic madness of the created universe."

If God argues for his own non-existence in the Book of Job, then Žižek believes that this is ritually fulfilled in the Crucifixion. Bearing in mind his philosophy that "there is no big Other", Žižek believes that the true philosophical lesson to be drawn from the story of the Crucifixion is not only that the son of God died on the Cross, but so did God, too.

167

Quantum uncertainty

Without a God, or indeed any figure of a big Other to fill out the subject's sense of individual and social identity, "reality" itself is rendered somehow incomplete and unfinished.

THIS VIEW OF "REALITY" AS ONTOLOGICALLY* UNFINISHED IS SOMETHING WITH WHICH CONTEMPORARY PHYSICS IS CONCERNED.

Quantum physics asserts that it is not possible to have full knowledge of particles at their quantum level, since the velocity and position of a particle cannot be described together.

*Ontology: the study of being and the nature of existence.

For **Albert Einstein** (1879–1955), this principle proved that quantum physics does not provide the full description of reality, and this led him to conclude that there must be some unknown features that escape quantum physics. However, subsequent physicists, such as **Werner Heisenberg** (1901–76) and **Niels Bohr** (1885–1962), believed otherwise.

WE INSIST THAT THIS INCOMPLETENESS OF OUR KNOWLEDGE OF QUANTUM REALITY POINTS TO A STRANGE INCOMPLETENESS OF QUANTUM REALITY ...

... AND THAT REALITY ITSELF IS ONTOLOGICALLY INCOMPLETE.

Digital reality

Žižek likens these physicists' view of reality to the digitally simulated reality of video games. The builders of such games do not bother to construct an *entire* reality. Certain parts of the game are constructed more fully than other parts. Parts that are not vital to the operation of the game – say, for instance, a house in the background – are not composed in their entirety. The same applies to the construction of a person, where to be convincing it is necessary only to construct the *outside* of the person.

IT IS POSSIBLE TO CONCEIVE OF THE UNIVERSE'S CONSTRUCTION IN SIMILAR TERMS.

Returning to a theological perspective, Žižek jokingly imagines God as a computer programmer who programmed our experience of reality. In this scenario, God is a slightly lazy programmer!

GOD DIDN'T FINISH THE PROJECT AND LEFT THINGS INCOMPLETE AT A QUANTUM LEVEL.

GOD THOUGHT THAT HUMANS WOULDN'T REACH FURTHER IN THEIR UNDERSTANDING THAN THE ATOMIC LEVEL.

BUT WE WERE A BIT TOO INTELLIGENT AND WENT BEYOND WHAT GOD HAD ANTICIPATED AND DISCOVERED THE INCOMPLETENESS OF HIS CREATION!

The freedom of an unfinished reality

Žižek finds this idea of the incompleteness of reality deeply liberating. In the absence of a complete "reality" the illusion of the self also collapses, since there is nothing definite existing in "outside reality" to help substantiate the coordinates of a self. All that is left is a confrontation with the fiction that lies at the heart of the symbolic order, but which the subject, in an effort to maintain a sense of unified identity, denies.

Further Reading

Chosen from some 50 published books, the following is a selective list of Žižek's writings that give a rounded view in chronological order of the different facets of his work and ideas. These range over politics, ideology, psychoanalysis and philosophy, frequently explored through subjects in both high and popular culture:

The Sublime Object of Ideology, Verso, 1989
Looking Awry: An Introduction to Jacques Lacan through Popular Culture, MIT Press, 1991
For They Know Not What They Do: Enjoyment as a Political Factor, Verso, 1991
Enjoy Your Symptom! Jacques Lacan In Hollywood and Out, Routledge, 1992 (second edition with an added chapter on *The Matrix*, 2000)
The Metastases of Enjoyment: Six Essays on Woman and Causality, Verso, 1994
The Indivisible Remainder: An Essay on Schelling and Related Matters, Verso, 1996
The Ticklish Subject: The Absent Centre of Political Ontology, Verso, 1999
Did Somebody Say Totalitarianism? Five Essays in the (Mis)Use of a Notion, Verso, 2001
On Belief, Routledge, 2001
Opera's Second Death (with Mladen Dolar), Routledge, 2002
The Puppet and the Dwarf: The Perverse Core of Christianity, MIT Press, 2003
The Parallax View, MIT Press, 2006
How to Read Lacan, Verso, 2007
In Defence of Lost Causes, Verso, 2007
First as Tragedy, Then as Farce, Verso, 2009
Living in the End Times, Verso, 2010

Speaking about his own writing, Žižek himself rates *The Sublime Object of Ideology*, *The Ticklish Subject* and *The Parallax View* as his finest books; also, *Opera's Second Death*, in which he focuses on Wagner's operas, is a book of which Žižek is particularly proud. Žižek's books are often brilliant works of virtuosity, although they can be conceptually complex and demanding – the introductory essays to *Slavoj Žižek Presents Robespierre: Virtue and Terror*, Verso, 2007, *Slavoj Žižek Presents Mao: On Practice and Contradiction*, Verso, 2007 and V.I. Lenin, *Revolution at the Gates: A Selection of Writings From 1917*, edited by Slavoj Žižek, Verso, 2002 provide short, pithy insights into Žižek's thinking and approach. *The Žižek Reader*, edited by Elizabeth Wright and Edmond Wright, Blackwell, 1999 also contains a selection of essays by Žižek divided into the topics of Culture, Woman and Philosophy.

Another way into Žižek is through the documentaries that have been made about him: *Žižek!*, directed by Astra Taylor and distributed by Zeitgeist films, was produced in 2005, and *The Pervert's Guide to Cinema*, 2006, was directed by Sophie Fiennes and scripted by Žižek (distributed by P. Guide Ltd and ICA Projects (UK)). Numerous videos of Žižek's lectures and talks are on YouTube and the web, and these are extremely illuminating and engaging. A full bibliography of Žižek's books as well as articles, compiled by the journal *lacanian ink*, is at http://www.lacan.com/bibliographyzi.htm. This site also lists some key secondary sources on Žižek. Matthew Sharpe and Geoff Boucher, *Žižek and Politics: A Critical Introduction*, Edinburgh University Press, 2010 is a well edited textbook outlining different understandings of Žižek's philosophical development and views.

Author's acknowledgements

I would like to thank all of the people who contributed to the preparation of this book, especially Duncan Heath, Piero, Dr Dean Kenning, Catherine Yass and the Masters students at the Byam Shaw School of Art at Central St Martins. In addition, Slavoj Žižek's extremely generous assistance in the early stages of the book's development was greatly appreciated by both Piero and me. I dedicate this book to my daughter, Enna Thea.

Extracts from Slavoj Žižek, *Looking Awry: An Introduction to Jacques Lacan through Popular Culture*, courtesy of MIT Press.

Christopher Kul-Want is leader of the Masters in Research in Art Theory and Philosophy course at Central St Martins College of Art and Design, University of the Arts, London. His books in Icon's *Introducing* series include *Introducing Kant* (1996), *Introducing Aesthetics* (2007) and *Introducing Continental Philosophy* (2012). He is the editor of *Philosophers on Art, From Kant to the Postmodernists: A Critical Reader* (Columbia University Press, 2010).

Piero is an illustrator, artist and graphic designer. He has also illustrated guides to the following subjects in the *Introducing* series: *Aesthetics*, *Anthropology*, *Barthes*, *Capitalism*, *Nietzsche*, *Psychiatry* and *Shakespeare*.

Index